Healing After Infidelity

A Step-by-Step Guide to Rebuilding Trust and Intimacy in Your Relationship

Jeffrey D. Murrah

Restore The Family Press

Contents

  Why the Affair Recovery Workshop is the Essential Companion to this Book
  Real Testimonials from Transformed Lives
  Your Journey to a Stronger Marriage Starts Here
  What You'll Receive:

Part I: Understanding Infidelity

Restore The Family Press

Chapter One

Finding Hope in the Darkness

The Unspoken Pain

Infidelity. The word alone evokes a whirlwind of emotions – pain, anger, betrayal, and disbelief. If you're reading this book, you or someone you love has likely experienced the devastating impact of an affair. You're not alone. Studies suggest that infidelity affects up to 40% of marriages, leaving countless couples grappling with the aftermath of shattered trust and broken promises.

The discovery of an affair can feel like the end of the world as if the very foundation of your relationship has crumbled beneath your feet. The pain is visceral, the anger all-consuming, and the path forward uncertain. In the midst of this chaos, it's easy to feel lost, hopeless, and alone.

A Glimmer of Hope

When Sarah first discovered that her husband, Michael, had been unfaithful, she felt like her entire world had crumbled. The pain was so raw and all-consuming that she couldn't imagine ever finding her way back to a place of trust and love. She did not believe she could ever forgive her husband for what he did. However, as she began to work through the exercises and strategies outlined in this book, Sarah slowly began to see hope on the horizon.

Your Roadmap to Healing

"Healing After Infidelity" is more than just a book – it's a companion, a guide, and a beacon of light in the darkness of betrayal. As a therapist who has worked with hundreds of couples struggling to recover from an affair, I've poured my heart and soul into creating a resource that can help you navigate this painful journey with compassion, wisdom, and hope.

This book distills the insights, strategies, and tools that have helped countless couples navigate the rocky terrain of infidelity and emerge stronger, wiser, and more deeply connected. It's not a magic formula or a quick fix but rather a compassionate, step-by-step guide to the hard work of healing.

In the following chapters, we'll explore the different types of affairs and their unique challenges. We'll explore practical individual and couple healing strategies, using real-life examples and anecdotes to illustrate key concepts. At the end of each chapter, you'll find reflection questions and exercises designed to help you personalize the lessons and apply them to your own situation.

The Path Forward

As you embark on this healing journey, know you are not alone. The path ahead may be rocky at times, but with patience, dedicated commitment, practice, and the right tools, you can emerge stronger and more resilient from this crisis than ever. So take a deep breath, turn the page, and begin this voyage of discovery and transformation together.

Reflection Questions:

1. What feelings and concerns are coming up for you as you begin this healing journey? Write your thoughts in a journal or share them with your partner, a trusted friend, or a therapist.

2. What do you hope to gain from reading this book and working through the exercises? Set an intention for your healing process and revisit it often to stay focused and motivated. The many feelings and memories can be distracting and keep you from your goals.

3. How can you create a supportive environment for yourself and your partner as you navigate this process? Brainstorm ideas for self-care, couple time, and outside support.

Chapter Two

The Landscape of Betrayal

Infidelity is not a singular, monolithic experience. Just as every relationship is unique, so are the circumstances and consequences of an affair. Understanding the different types of infidelity and the specific challenges each presents is a crucial first step in the healing process.

The Betrayal of the One-Night Stand

When Rachel's husband, David, came home late one night, smelling of unfamiliar perfume, she immediately knew something was wrong. After hours of painful questioning, David finally admitted to having a one-night stand with a coworker after an office party. While he insisted it meant nothing and would never happen again, Rachel was left reeling, her trust shattered in an instant.

A one-night stand is exactly what it sounds like – a single, isolated sexual encounter outside of the primary relationship. While some may dismiss this type of affair as "not a big deal," the betrayal of trust and the breach of monogamy can be just as devastating as a longer-term entanglement.

The unique challenge of a one-night stand lies in its brevity. Because the encounter was short-lived, the unfaithful partner may be tempted to downplay its significance or sweep it under the rug. They may use phrases like "It didn't mean anything" or "It was just sex," failing to recognize the deep emotional impact their actions have had on their partner or how their statements demean and diminish the intimacy they have shared with their spouse. In playing down the one-night stand, they weaken their marriage.

For the betrayed partner, a one-night stand can trigger intense feelings of inadequacy, rejection, and even disgust. They may obsess over the details of the encounter, wondering what they could have done differently to prevent it. The fact that the affair was fleeting does not negate the pain it causes.

In situations where there are a series of one-night stands, it raises the possibility of a sexual addiction.

The Slow Burn of the Long-Term Affair

For years, Sophie had a nagging feeling that something wasn't quite right in her marriage to James. He constantly worked late, took mysterious phone calls, and seemed emotionally distant. When she finally discovered that James had been carrying on a long-term affair with his high school sweetheart, Sophie felt like her entire life had been a lie.

On the other end of the affair spectrum are long-term affairs – relationships that develop over months or even years, often involving deep emotional connections and elaborate deceptions. These affairs are particularly insidious because they often involve a gradual erosion of boundaries and a slow, steady diversion of time, energy, and affection away from the primary relationship.

The betrayed partner in a long-term affair may feel like they've been living a lie, that the entire foundation of their relationship has been called into question. They may wonder how they could have missed the signs for so long or feel foolish for trusting their partner so completely. With long-term affairs, some accommodations have been made whether or not those involved are consciously aware of them.

For the unfaithful partner, ending a long-term affair can be a wrenching experience in and of itself. They may grieve the loss of the affair partner and struggle with feelings of guilt, shame, and confusion as they try to recommit to their primary relationship.

The Gray Area of Emotional Affairs

When Mark started confiding in his coworker, Emily, about his marital problems, he never intended for it to turn into anything more. But as their conversations became more intimate and he found himself looking forward to their daily chats more than coming home to his wife, Mark realized he was in the midst of an emotional affair. His affair partner, in this case, believed she was helping him and providing understanding that he was not receiving at home.

Not all affairs involve physical intimacy. An emotional affair is characterized by a deep, intimate connection with someone outside the primary relationship, often at the expense of emotional intimacy with one's partner. These affairs can be just as damaging as sexual infidelity, if not more so.

The unique challenge of emotional affairs lies in their ambiguity. Because there is no clear line crossed, like with sexual infidelity, the unfaithful partner may be in denial about the inappropriateness of their behavior. They may insist that they're "just friends" with the affair partner, failing to recognize the depth of their emotional investment. This sets the stage for gaslighting and dismissing the concerns as 'overreacting.'

For the betrayed partner, an emotional affair can feel like a rejection of their entire being. They may feel like they're not enough, that they're lacking in some fundamental way that drove their partner to seek emotional fulfillment elsewhere.

The Digital Age of Online Affairs and Sexting

When Jenna stumbled upon a string of explicit messages on her husband's social media account, she was floored. Tom had been engaging in online sexting and virtual affairs with multiple women, all while sitting right next to Jenna on the couch.

Online affairs and sexting have become increasingly common, with the anonymity and accessibility of the internet making it all too easy to blur the lines of fidelity. Online affairs can involve everything from flirtatious messaging and emotional disclosure to explicit sexual communication and even virtual sex acts.

The unique challenge of online affairs and sexting is the ease and accessibility of these interactions. With just a few clicks, individuals can connect with affair partners from anywhere in the world, any time of day or night. The privacy and anonymity of these digital spaces can create a false sense of disconnection from real-world consequences.

For the betrayed partner, discovering an online affair can be a shocking violation of trust. They may feel like their partner has been living a double life, presenting one face to them while engaging in intimate exchanges with strangers online.

Navigating the Complexities

Regardless of the specific form an affair takes, the pain of betrayal is universal. However, understanding the unique dynamics and challenges of each type of infidelity can be an important part of the healing process.

By recognizing the specific wounds caused by a one-night stand versus a long-term entanglement or an emotional affair versus a digital dalliance, couples can develop a more targeted, effective recovery plan. They can also address the anxieties, triggers, and trust issues arising from their unique situation.

It's also important to acknowledge that affairs often exist on a continuum and involve elements of multiple categories. An emotional affair may escalate into a physical one, and a series of one-night stands may develop into a longer-term entanglement. The goal is not to pigeonhole or label but rather to understand the full complexity of the situation.

As you reflect on your own experience with infidelity, consider the specific type or types of betrayal you're grappling with. What unique challenges do you face as a result? How has your understanding of the affair evolved as you've learned more about its nature and extent?

No matter what form the affair took, your pain is real, and your healing matters. By facing the reality of the betrayal head-on and committing to the hard work of recovery, you're already taking brave, important steps toward a brighter future.

Reflection Questions:

1. Reflect on the specific type or types of infidelity that have impacted your relationship. How has this particular kind of betrayal

affected you emotionally, mentally, and physically?

2. Write about a specific moment when you realized the extent or nature of the affair. What thoughts and feelings come up as you revisit this moment?

3. How has your understanding of the affair changed over time? What new insights or discoveries have you made about your situation and its unique challenges?

Chapter Three

The Whys Behind the Lies

The Perfect Storm

Karen and Jack's Story

When Karen first met her husband, Jack, she was drawn to his charming smile and quick wit. However, as the years passed, Karen noticed a change in Jack's behavior. He became withdrawn, moody, and increasingly critical of their relationship. When she discovered he had been having an affair with a coworker, Karen was devastated – but not entirely surprised.

As Karen and Jack began to unpack the factors that had contributed to the affair, they realized it was not a single event but a culmination of years of unmet needs, poor communication, and growing resentment. Jack had been struggling with untreated depression and had turned to the affair as a way to cope with his feelings of inadequacy and disconnection. Karen, in turn, had been so focused on her career and their children that she had neglected her emotional needs and the intimacy in their marriage.

Through therapy and honest conversation, Karen and Jack began to understand how their individual struggles and the dynamics in their relationship had created a perfect storm for infidelity to occur. They worked to address Jack's depression, improve their communication skills, and prioritize their emotional and physical intimacy. Gradually, they were able to weather the storm and rebuild a stronger, more resilient marriage.

The Lessons

Infidelity often arises from a complex combination of factors rather than a single, isolated cause. Just as a perfect storm in nature results from a rare confluence of meteorological events, the perfect storm of an affair is typically the result of multiple intersecting forces like the situation with Karen and Jack.

These forces can include long-standing relationship issues, such as communication breakdowns, emotional disconnection, or mismatched expectations. They may also involve individual vulnerabilities, such as untreated mental health issues, low self-esteem, or unresolved trauma. External stressors, such as job loss, financial strain, or health problems, can also contribute to the overall climate of the relationship, creating a sense of disconnection or vulnerability.

The perfect storm analogy emphasizes the idea that infidelity is rarely a simple, straightforward event. It's a complex, multifaceted phenomenon that arises from a unique combination of factors specific to each couple and individual. By understanding the various forces at play, couples can develop a more nuanced, compassionate approach to healing and avoid the trap of oversimplification or blame.

Each spouse brings baggage into their marriage. Coupled with pressures and temptations, that baggage can create a perfect storm situation. Each spouse likely has a different view of the events and their significance.

Echoes of the Past

Sarah's Story

As a child, Sarah witnessed her father's repeated infidelities and the toll they took on her mother. She swore she would never put her own family through that kind of pain. But when Sarah found herself drawn into an affair with a close friend, she realized she had been subconsciously replicating the patterns she had learned growing up. The guilt of putting her family through what she experienced as a child left her devastated.

Through therapy, Sarah began to understand how her early experiences had shaped her beliefs about love, intimacy, and relationships. She realized that she had internalized a fear of abandonment and a belief that she was unworthy of faithful, committed love. The committed love of her husband left her feeling unworthy as if she did not deserve him. To deal with these feelings, she sought out an affair partner who would leave her feeling uncertain. These echoes of the past had led her to seek validation and security through the affair, even as it threatened to destroy the very family she had vowed to protect.

As Sarah worked to heal her own wounds and break free from the patterns of her past, she also began to rebuild trust and intimacy with her husband. She learned to communicate her fears and needs openly and to seek the love and security she craved within her marriage. Gradually, Sarah was able to create a new legacy for her family – one of faithfulness, honesty, and resilience. She also learned to accept love, even when she felt unworthy.

The Lessons

Unresolved trauma and past relationship wounds can create a ripple effect, influencing an individual's behavior and choices in their current relationship. Just as an echo reflects a past sound, the echoes of the past refer to how our early experiences and relationship patterns can reverberate through our present lives.

For some individuals, the experience of neglect, abandonment, or betrayal in their early relationships creates a subconscious template for future interactions. They may find themselves drawn to partners who recreate familiar dynamics, even if those dynamics are ultimately harmful or unfulfilling. An affair may be an unconscious attempt to heal old wounds, fill emotional voids, or gain a sense of control or validation that was lacking in early life. A popular term for this is 'trauma bonds.'

The echoes of the past can also manifest in attachment styles and coping mechanisms. Individuals with insecure attachment styles, often developed in response to inconsistent or unreliable caregiving, may struggle with intimacy, trust, and communication in their adult relationships. They may turn to infidelity as a way to avoid vulnerability, maintain a sense of independence, or preemptively protect themselves from abandonment.

By exploring past traumas, individuals can gain insight into the deeper, often unconscious, patterns and motivations that may have contributed to the affair. When the attraction does not make sense, it could very likely be the influence of a trauma bond. This awareness can be a powerful catalyst for healing, growth, and change, allowing individuals to break free from the echoes of the past and create healthier, more fulfilling relationships in the present.

The Lure of the New

Mark and Rachel's Story

Mark loved his wife, Rachel, but after 15 years of marriage, he couldn't shake the feeling that something was missing. When a new coworker started flirting with him, Mark felt a rush of excitement and vitality he hadn't experienced in years. Before he knew it, he was in the throes of a passionate affair, chasing the high of novelty and forbidden desire.

As the affair progressed, however, Mark realized that the excitement was more about escaping his own restlessness and dissatisfaction than genuinely connecting with his new partner. He missed the depth and history he shared with Rachel and felt increasingly guilty about the pain he was causing her.

With the help of a therapist, Mark and Rachel were able to have honest conversations about the factors that had led to the affair. They realized they had neglected their relationship and took each other for granted. They committed to adding more novelty, excitement, and intimacy into their marriage through regular date nights, new shared hobbies, and open communication about their needs and desires. They needed to include fun and play. As they worked to rebuild trust and connection, they discovered a newfound appreciation for the love and history they shared.

Mark realized he had been so totally out of touch with his emotions that he could not identify and label them. The affair was not about love, caring, or affection. In his case, it was a new sensation lacking the emotional depth he had with Rachel.

The Lessons

The powerful allure of novelty plays a significant role in the development of an affair. Just as a shiny new object can capture our attention and excite our senses, the lure of a new romantic interest can be a potent force, particularly for individuals who feel stuck, stagnant, or unfulfilled in their primary relationship.

A rush of feel-good chemicals, such as dopamine, norepinephrine, and serotonin, often characterizes the early stages of a new relationship. These chemicals can create a sense of euphoria, intensity, and obsessive preoccupation that can be highly addictive. For individuals who have been in a long-term relationship, the novelty of a new partner can provide a thrilling contrast to the familiarity and routine of their established partnership.

The excitement of secrecy and taboo can also fuel the lure of the new. The illicit nature of an affair can add an element of danger and transgression that can be a powerful aphrodisiac for some individuals. The need for secrecy can create a sense of shared intimacy and specialness, further fueling the intensity of the new connection.

It's important to note that the lure of the new is often more about escaping the self than genuinely connecting with another person. The new partner may represent an idealized version of love or a projection of unfulfilled desires rather than a fully realized individual with their own needs and flaws. As the novelty fades and reality sets in, the affair may lose its luster, leaving the unfaithful partner feeling disillusioned and disconnected.

By understanding the seductive power of novelty and the underlying needs it may be attempting to meet, couples can work to create a sense of excitement, vitality, and growth within their primary relationship. They can inject novelty, surprise, and adventure into their partnership while cultivating a deeper sense of emotional intimacy and connection.

The Pressure Cooker

John and Emily's Story

From the outside, John and Emily's marriage looked picture-perfect. But behind closed doors, the pressure to maintain an image of success and happiness took a toll. John worked long hours to provide for his family, while Emily felt increasingly lonely and resentful. When a chance encounter with an old flame reignited a spark, Emily turned to the affair as an escape from the suffocating expectations of her life.

As the affair came to light, John and Emily were forced to confront how they had been living separate lives and the toll that the pressure to maintain appearances had taken on their relationship. Through therapy, they began to communicate honestly about their feelings of overwhelm, resentment, and disconnection. They set boundaries around work and family time and committed to prioritizing their relationship over external measures of success.

Gradually, John and Emily were able to let go of the pressure to be perfect and embrace a more authentic, connected way of being together. They found ways to support each other's needs and desires while nurturing their bond as a couple. As they learned to be more vulnerable and honest with each other, they discovered a deeper level of intimacy and happiness than they had ever known before.

The Lessons

Societal pressures and expectations can create a pressure cooker environment in relationships, leading some individuals to seek outlets for stress and dissatisfaction through infidelity. Just as a pressure cooker uses high pressure to cook food quickly, the pressure cooker of modern life can create a sense of intense, unrelenting stress that can strain even the strongest relationships.

In our achievement-oriented culture, there is often immense pressure to maintain an image of success, happiness, and perfection. Couples may feel pressure to have the perfect marriage, the perfect family, the perfect career, and the perfect lifestyle. The fear of being seen as a failure or the shame of admitting to struggles can lead individuals to put on a façade of contentment while secretly struggling with feelings of inadequacy, resentment, or despair.

The pressure to meet these unrealistic expectations can create a sense of disconnection and isolation within the relationship. Partners may feel like they can't be honest about their struggles or vulnerabilities, leading to a breakdown in communication and emotional intimacy. They may turn to an affair as a way to escape the pressure, find validation, or experience a sense of autonomy and control.

The pressure cooker of modern life can also create practical challenges that strain the relationship. Long work hours, financial stress, and the demands of parenting can leave partners feeling exhausted, overwhelmed, and disconnected. The lack of quality time together can create a sense of emotional distance and make it easier for one or both partners to seek connection and fulfillment outside the relationship.

By recognizing the impact of societal pressures and expectations on the relationship, couples can work to create a more authentic, supportive, and resilient partnership. They can learn to communicate honestly about their struggles, set realistic expectations, and prioritize their connection and well-being over external measures of success. They can also find healthy ways to manage stress and cultivate a sense of shared purpose and meaning within the relationship.

Peeling Back the Layers

It's important to approach the reasons behind an affair with curiosity, compassion, and a willingness to explore the complex, multilayered factors that may have contributed to the situation. Just as an onion has many layers that must be peeled back to reach the core, understanding the true reasons behind an affair often requires a process of deep, intentional exploration.

It's common for couples to seek a single, clear-cut explanation for an affair, such as a character flaw in the unfaithful partner or a specific unmet need in the relationship. However, the reality is often much more nuanced and multifaceted. An affair is typically the result of a complex interplay of individual, relational, and contextual factors, each layer influencing and compounding the others.

By peeling back the layers and exploring the deeper roots of the affair, couples can move beyond simplistic explanations and develop a more comprehensive, empathetic understanding of the situation. They can explore questions such as:

- Were there long-standing issues in the relationship, such as poor communication, emotional disconnection, or mismatched expectations, that created a sense of vulnerability or dissatisfaction?

- Did either partner struggle with untreated mental health issues, addiction, or unresolved trauma that influenced their behavior or coping mechanisms?

- Were there significant life stressors or transitions, such as job loss, financial strain, or the birth of a child, that put additional pressure on the relationship?

- Did either partner have a history of infidelity or unresolved pain from past relationships that may have influenced their choices or reactions?

Peeling back the layers requires a willingness to be vulnerable, honest, and self-reflective. It may involve difficult conversations, uncomfortable realizations, and a readiness to confront long-standing patterns or beliefs. However, by engaging in this process with openness and compassion, couples can better understand themselves, their partner, and their relationship.

This level of understanding can be a powerful catalyst for healing and growth. It can help the betrayed partner move beyond blame and victimhood, recognizing that the affair was not a reflection of their worth or lovability. It can provide a framework for forgiveness and a pathway to rebuilding trust and intimacy. It can help the unfaithful partner take responsibility for their actions while developing greater insight into their needs, vulnerabilities, and growth areas.

Ultimately, peeling back the layers is about developing a more complex, nuanced, compassionate understanding of the human experience. It's about recognizing that we are all imperfect, multifaceted beings shaped by a complex web of experiences, relationships, and contexts. By approaching the aftermath of an affair with this level of depth and empathy, couples can lay the groundwork for profound healing, growth, and transformation.

Reflection Questions:

1. Looking back, were there any warning signs or red flags that the relationship was vulnerable to an affair? What unmet needs or long-standing issues may have contributed to the situation?

2. Has either partner struggled with mental health issues, addiction, or unresolved trauma that may have played a role in the infidelity? How might addressing these underlying issues support the healing process?

3. Were there any external pressures or stressors that may have created a sense of disconnection or vulnerability in the relationship? How can you work together to create a more supportive, resilient partnership moving forward?

Chapter Four

The Aftermath of Discovery

The Emotional Earthquake

Jessica and David's Story

When Jessica stumbled upon a string of intimate text messages between her husband, David, and another woman, she felt like the ground had fallen beneath her feet. In an instant, the life she had known and the future she had envisioned lay in ruins. She confronted David, who admitted to the affair, and Jessica found herself plunged into a world of rage, despair, and disbelief.

In the following days and weeks, Jessica struggled to make sense of her new reality. She oscillated between fits of anger, bouts of uncontrollable crying, and periods of eerie numbness. She couldn't eat, sleep, or imagine how she would ever trust David again. The shock of the discovery had left her reeling, and she felt utterly alone in her pain.

The emotional episodes and lack of self-care made her look like another woman than the one in the wedding photographs.

The Lessons

The initial discovery of an affair can be one of the most traumatic and emotionally devastating experiences a person can go through. It's common to feel as if your entire world has been shattered and to experience a wide range of intense, sometimes contradictory emotions. Shock, anger, sadness, fear, and disbelief are all normal reactions to the profound betrayal of infidelity. It's important to remember that these feelings are valid and that everyone processes the trauma of an affair in their own way and at their own pace.

Jessica's not eating made the situation worse. She found herself reacting rather than thinking. Her body and brain were not receiving the nutrients they needed to function properly. The shock of an affair is bad enough. When combined with not eating, the sensation of being out of control is more pronounced. She felt at the mercy of everything going on around her.

The Roller-coaster of Reactions

Sarah and Mark's Story

When Sarah learned of her husband Mark's infidelity, her first reaction was a kind of eerie calm. She listened quietly as Mark confessed to the affair, nodding along as if she were hearing about someone else's life. It wasn't until several hours later, as she was mindlessly chopping vegetables for dinner, that the reality of the situation hit her. The knife clattered to the floor, and Sarah collapsed into sobs that left her gasping for breath.

In the weeks that followed, Sarah found herself on an emotional roller-coaster. Some days, she would wake up feeling almost normal, as if the affair had been a bad dream. She was consumed by rage on other days, lashing out at Mark for his betrayal. Still, other times, she was gripped by despair so deep that she could barely get out of bed. She worried that she was losing her mind, that she would never feel like herself again.

The extremes in her moods and behavior led others to ask if she was "okay." On her 'good days, ' she seemed like her old self, yet all it took was a comment or reminder, and her mind started racing. Thoughts of what Mark did and what she imagined happened tormented her and took her to the other extreme.

The Lessons

The aftermath of discovering an affair can be a time of intense emotional upheaval and extremes. It's common to experience a wide range of reactions, sometimes cycling through them rapidly and unpredictably. You may feel numb one moment and overwhelmed with anger or sadness the next. You may have intrusive thoughts or images related to the affair or find yourself obsessively replaying certain moments or conversations in your mind.

These reactions are a normal part of processing the trauma of infidelity. It's important to allow yourself to feel your feelings without judgment and to find healthy ways to express and cope with them. This might involve journaling, talking to a trusted friend or therapist, or engaging in physical activities that help release pent-up emotions. Remember that healing is a process and that taking things one day, one hour, or even one minute at a time is okay.

The Importance of Self-Care

Emily's Story

When Emily discovered her girlfriend Jenna's affair, her first instinct was to push away her own pain and focus on fixing the relationship. She threw herself into couples therapy, read every book on infidelity she could find, and tried to be the perfect, understanding partner. However, as the weeks wore on, Emily became physically and emotionally more exhausted.

It wasn't until her therapist gently pointed out that Emily was neglecting her own needs that she realized how little she had been taking care of herself. She skipped meals, neglected her hobbies, and isolated herself from friends and family. With her therapist's encouragement, Emily began to prioritize self-care. She started setting aside time each day for activities that brought her joy and comfort, like taking long walks in nature or savoring a cup of her favorite tea. She reached out to loved ones for support and began attending a weekly support group for partners of unfaithful spouses.

As Emily started to take better care of herself, she found that she had more energy and emotional capacity to deal with the challenges of healing from the affair. She was able to approach the situation with greater clarity and compassion, both for herself and for Jenna. And while the road ahead was still long, Emily felt more equipped to handle the journey.

The Lessons

In the aftermath of discovering an affair, it can be easy to neglect your own needs and well-being. You may be so focused on trying to understand what happened, save your relationship, or support your partner that you forget to take care of yourself. But self-care is crucial to the healing process. By prioritizing your physical, emotional, and spiritual needs, you give yourself the strength and resilience to weather the challenges ahead.

Self-care can take many forms, and what works for one person may not work for another. Some common practices include:

- Getting enough rest, eating nourishing meals regularly

- Engaging in physical activities that reduce stress and promote well-being, such as swimming, weight lifting, running, yoga, or time in nature

- Seeking support from trusted friends, family members, or a therapist

- Pursuing hobbies or activities that bring joy and fulfillment

- Practicing mindfulness or other relaxation techniques to manage difficult emotions

Remember that caring for yourself is not selfish – it's a necessary part of the healing process. By filling your cup, you put yourself in a better position to navigate the challenges of recovery and show up as your best self, both for yourself and your relationship. When you look like a mess, it demotivates your spouse from returning to you. You want them to desire to be with you and enjoy your company.

The Road Ahead

Discovering an affair can be a life-altering event, one that shatters your sense of trust, security, and identity. The emotional aftermath can be intense, overwhelming, and sometimes all-consuming. But as painful as this experience is, know that you are not alone and that healing is possible.

By allowing yourself to feel your feelings, seeking support, and prioritizing self-care, you give yourself the best chance of navigating this difficult chapter with resilience and grace. In the coming sections, we'll explore strategies for processing the trauma of infidelity, rebuilding trust and intimacy, and ultimately, finding your way back to wholeness and joy.

Reflection Questions:

1. What has been the hardest part of the emotional aftermath of discovering the affair? What feelings or reactions have surprised or challenged you the most?

2. Who are the trusted friends, family members, or professionals you can turn to for support during this time? How can you communicate your needs and ask for help when needed?

3. What self-care practices feel most nourishing and supportive to you right now? How can you prioritize these activities, even when life feels overwhelming or chaotic?

4. Are you eating meals that help you think clearly and give you energy throughout the day? Are you binging or starving yourself?

Part II: Healing as Individuals

Restore The Family Press

Chapter Five

Strategies for the Betrayed Partner

When you've been betrayed by your partner, the pain can feel all-consuming. You may struggle with a whirlwind of emotions – anger, sadness, confusion, and despair – that threaten to overwhelm you at every turn. The road to healing can feel long and daunting but know that you are not alone and that recovery is possible. In this chapter, we'll explore strategies for making sense of the trauma of infidelity, rebuilding your sense of self, and, ultimately, finding your way back to wholeness and peace.

The Weight of Betrayal

Lauren's Story

When Lauren discovered that her husband of 15 years had been having an affair with a coworker, she felt as if her entire world had crumbled. She couldn't eat or sleep and barely functioned at work. The pain of the betrayal consumed her every waking thought, and she found herself replaying every moment of their relationship, searching for signs she had missed.

As the weeks turned into months, Lauren began to realize that the affair had not only shattered her trust in her husband but also her trust in herself. She questioned her judgment, desirability, and worth as a partner. The weight of the betrayal had left her feeling broken and alone, and she wasn't sure how to begin picking up the pieces. Questions went through her head like "Who would want you?" and "What makes you think you are desirable?"

The Lessons

The trauma of infidelity can be all-encompassing, affecting every aspect of your life and sense of self. It's common to experience a wide range of intense emotions, including anger, sadness, fear, and confusion. You may find yourself obsessing over details of the affair, questioning your own worth and desirability, and struggling to imagine a future beyond the pain.

When you are in pain, it feels like time slows down. The pain also makes any thoughts about the future seem distant and far away. The pain forces your focus to change. You now only think about your own hurts.

Remembering these feelings are a normal response to a profoundly abnormal situation is important. You are not weak, broken, or deficient in experiencing them. The betrayal you have suffered reflects your partner's choices, not your worth as a person. As you begin the process of healing, be gentle with yourself and allow yourself to feel your feelings without judgment. As you begin healing, you gain a better sense of having a future and having some hope.

Processing the Trauma

Shannon's Story

In the months following the discovery of her partner's infidelity, Shannon tried to push away her pain and carry on as if nothing had happened. She threw herself into her work, children, and social life, hoping her heartache would fade if she just stayed busy enough. But the more she tried to ignore her feelings, the more they festered, bubbling up in unexpected ways – panic attacks, fits of rage, and a deep, unshakeable sadness. In those moments of rage, she had thoughts of revenge and finding ways of hurting others back.

It wasn't until Shannon began working with a therapist that she realized the importance of processing her trauma in a healthy way. With her therapist's guidance, Shannon began to allow herself to feel the full depth of her pain, anger, and grief.

She learned self-soothing and emotional regulation techniques, such as deep breathing, meditation, and journaling. She started to understand that healing was not a linear process but rather a series of small, sometimes messy steps forward. She also realized there would be good days and not-so-good days. The journaling helped her identify the triggers that set her off.

The meditation helped calm her mind when ugly thoughts of revenge arose, and the self-soothing helped calm her down when the tension made her feel like she was at the end of her rope.

The Lessons

Processing the trauma of infidelity is a crucial step in the healing journey. It's not about "getting over" the pain or pushing it away, but rather learning to sit with it, understand it, and ultimately integrate it into your story in a way that allows you to move forward.

There is no one-size-fits-all approach to processing betrayal trauma, but some common strategies include:

- Seeking the support of a qualified therapist who specializes in infidelity recovery

- Joining a support group for betrayed partners to connect with others who understand your experience

- Practicing self-care activities that promote emotional and physical well-being, such as exercise, meditation, or creative pursuits

- Allowing yourself to grieve the losses associated with the betrayal, such as the loss of trust, the loss of the relationship you thought you had, or the loss of your sense of safety and security

- Challenging negative self-talk and beliefs that may arise after the betrayal, such as "I'm not good enough" or "I'll never be able to trust again."

-Hurting others was not a healthy way of reducing her own pain.

Remember that working through trauma is a journey. That journey doesn't end when the pain stops; it ends when you are healed inside and out. Be patient with yourself and trust that with time, support, and self-compassion, you can heal and grow from this painful experience.

Rebuilding Self-Trust

Michael's Story

In the wake of his wife's affair, Michael found himself plagued by doubts and insecurities. He questioned his own judgment, wondering how he could have been so blind to the signs of her infidelity. He blamed himself for not being a good enough husband, for not being attractive or interesting enough to keep her attention. And he struggled to trust his own perceptions and intuition, constantly second-guessing himself and his decisions.

As Michael began working with a support group for betrayed spouses, he started to realize that rebuilding trust in himself was just as important as rebuilding trust in his wife. With the help of his fellow group members, Michael began to challenge the negative beliefs he held about himself and his role in the affair. He started setting small, achievable goals for himself – such as trying a new hobby or reaching out to a friend for support – and celebrating each accomplishment along the way.

Slowly but surely, Michael began to rediscover his own strength, resilience, and worth. He learned to trust his judgment again and recognize that his wife's choices did not reflect his value as a person. He started to see himself not as a victim of betrayal but as a survivor—someone who had been through a challenging time and come out the other side stronger and wiser.

The Lessons

One of the most devastating impacts of infidelity is the way it can shatter your sense of self-trust. You may find yourself questioning your own decision-making, your intuition, and your worth as a partner. You may blame yourself for not seeing the signs of the affair or for not being "enough" to keep your partner faithful.

Rebuilding self-trust is a crucial component of the healing process. It's about learning to trust your perceptions, value your needs and desires, and believe in your inherent worth and lovability. Some strategies for rebuilding self-trust include:

- Challenging negative self-talk and beliefs that may arise in the aftermath of the betrayal

- Setting small, achievable goals for yourself and celebrating each accomplishment along the way

- Surrounding yourself with supportive, affirming people who reflect on your strengths and value

- Practicing self-compassion and treating yourself with the same kindness and understanding you would extend to a dear friend

- Engaging in activities that promote self-discovery and personal growth, such as therapy, journaling, or creative pursuits

Remember that rebuilding self-trust is a gradual process, and setbacks are a normal part of the journey. Be patient with yourself and trust that with time and practice, you can cultivate a deep, unshakeable sense of self-worth and self-trust.

Setting Boundaries

Emily and Tom's Story

When Emily learned of her husband Tom's affair, she was consumed by a desire to understand every detail of the relationship. She demanded access to his phone and email, interrogated him about his whereabouts and intentions, and became increasingly controlling in her efforts to prevent another betrayal.

As the months wore on, however, Emily realized that her attempts to control Tom's behavior were ineffective and deeply damaging to her own well-being. She was exhausted from constantly policing his actions and felt trapped in a cycle of hyper-vigilance and fear. She considered hiring a private investigator and putting tracking devices on his car.

With the help of a therapist, Emily began to work on setting healthy boundaries in her relationship. She learned to communicate her needs and expectations clearly and calmly without resorting to demands or ultimatums. She started prioritizing her own self-care and well-being, carving out time for activities and relationships that brought her joy and fulfillment. And she began to understand that while she could not control Tom's choices, she could control her own responses and actions.

As Emily established clearer boundaries and expectations in her relationship, she felt more empowered and secure in herself. She was no longer consumed by the need to monitor Tom's every move and could focus on her own healing and growth. And while the process was not always easy, Emily discovered that setting boundaries was essential in rebuilding trust and intimacy in her marriage.

The Lessons

In the aftermath of infidelity, it's common to feel a desperate need to regain control over your relationship and your life. You may try to monitor your partner's every move, demanding constant reassurance and proof of their faithfulness. But while these impulses are understandable, they are ultimately unsustainable and can further erode trust and intimacy in the relationship.

Setting healthy boundaries is a crucial component of the healing process. It's about communicating your needs and expectations clearly and calmly while also respecting your own limits and well-being. Some strategies for setting boundaries after infidelity include:

- Identifying your non-negotiables – the behaviors and actions that are absolutely unacceptable to you in the relationship (for example, flirting with others, lunch with certain co-workers)

- Communicating your needs and expectations clearly and directly, without resorting to demands or ultimatums

- Prioritizing your own self-care and well-being and making time for activities and relationships that bring you joy and fulfillment

- Learning to trust your own instincts and judgments and refusing to tolerate behavior that violates your boundaries or values

- Seeking the support of a therapist or support group to help you navigate the challenges of setting and maintaining healthy boundaries

Setting boundaries is not about punishing your partner or seeking to control their behavior. Rather, it's about taking responsibility for your own well-being and creating a relationship dynamic that feels safe, respectful, and nurturing for both partners.

Navigating Triggers

Jessica's Story

Two years after her partner's affair, Jessica thought she had moved past the worst of the pain and betrayal. She had gone to therapy, worked on rebuilding trust with her partner, and felt like she was finally starting to heal. But one day, she discovered an old love note from her partner to the affair partner while cleaning out a closet. Suddenly, she was transported back to the moment of discovery, reliving all the heartache and trauma of the betrayal.

For days after the incident, Jessica struggled with intrusive thoughts and images related to the affair. She found herself snapping at her partner and children over small matters. It felt like all the progress she had made in her healing had been erased, and she was back at square one.

With the help of her therapist, Jessica began to understand that her reaction was a normal response to a triggering event. She learned strategies for managing triggers, such as grounding techniques, self-soothing practices, and open communication with her partner. She started to see that healing was a series of ups and downs, setbacks, and progress.

As Jessica continued to work on her recovery, she found that navigating triggers became easier over time. She learned to anticipate potential triggering situations and have a plan to cope with them. And she discovered that each time she faced a trigger and moved through it, she grew a little stronger and more resilient.

The Lessons

Triggers are a common and normal part of the healing process after infidelity. A trigger is any stimulus – a thought, image, smell, place, or experience – that reminds you of the betrayal and brings up painful emotions and memories. Triggers can be obvious, such as seeing your partner with the affair partner, or more subtle, such as hearing a song that reminds you of the time of the discovery.

Navigating triggers can be challenging, but some strategies can help. Some tips for managing triggers include:

- Identifying your triggers and developing a plan for coping with them when they arise

- Practicing grounding techniques, such as deep breathing or sensory awareness, to help you stay present and calm in the face of a trigger

- Communicating openly with your partner about your triggers and what you need from them in those moments

- Seeking the support of a therapist or support group to help you process and manage triggering experiences

- Practicing self-compassion and reminding yourself that triggers are a normal part of the healing process and not a sign of weakness or failure

It's important to remember that navigating triggers is a skill that develops over time. Be patient with yourself and trust that with practice and support, you can learn to move through triggering experiences with greater ease and resilience.

The Road Ahead

Healing from the trauma of infidelity is a deeply personal and individual journey. There is no one-size-fits-all approach or timeline for recovery. But by prioritizing your self-care, healthily processing your emotions, rebuilding self-trust, setting boundaries, and learning to navigate triggers, you can begin to move forward and reclaim your sense of self and well-being.

Setbacks and challenges are normal parts of the healing journey. Be gentle with yourself and surround yourself with supportive, compassionate people who can reflect on your worth and value. Trust that with time, effort, and self-compassion, you can emerge from this painful chapter stronger, wiser, and more resilient than ever before.

Reflection Questions:

1. What has been the most challenging aspect of processing the trauma of infidelity for you? What strategies or support systems have you found most helpful in coping with the pain and betrayal?

2. How has the infidelity impacted your sense of self-trust and self-worth? What steps can you take to rebuild trust in yourself and your judgment?

3. What boundaries do you need to set in your relationship to feel safe, respected, and valued moving forward? How can you communicate these needs and expectations to your partner clearly and assertively?

Chapter Six

Strategies for the Unfaithful Partner

If you are the unfaithful partner, the road ahead may feel daunting and uncertain. You may be grappling with feelings of guilt, shame, and confusion, unsure of how to begin repairing the damage your actions have caused, whether intentional or unforeseen. While there is no easy fix or quick solution, there are steps you can take to demonstrate your remorse, rebuild trust, and lay the foundation for a healthier, more honest relationship. In this chapter, we'll explore strategies for taking responsibility, unpacking your motivations, and, ultimately, doing the hard work of making amends.

The Weight of Responsibility

John's Story

When John's affair came to light, his first instinct was to minimize and defend his actions. He told his wife, Tammy, that it was *"just a fling"* and that it *"didn't mean anything."* He blamed the stress of his job, the lack of intimacy in their marriage, and even Tammy herself for not being attentive enough to his needs. But as the reality of the pain he had caused began to sink in, John realized that his defensiveness was only making things worse.

With the help of a therapist, John began to understand that taking responsibility for his actions was the first and most critical step in the healing process. He learned to stop making excuses and to own the choices he had made.

He sat with the discomfort of seeing the pain he had caused and resisted the urge to deflect or minimize. It took a while for him to see that his actions brought hurt in ways he never imagined. It hurt Tammy, her family, his family, and their friends. It brought shame to Tammy and left her feeling like she was unwanted and unattractive. John started to understand that true remorse wasn't just about saying "I'm sorry" but about being willing to do the hard work of repairing the damage he had done.

The Lessons

One of the most important things you can do as the unfaithful partner is to take full responsibility for your actions. This means acknowledging the hurt you have caused, owning your choices, and resisting the urge to make excuses or shift blame. It's natural to want to defend yourself or minimize the impact of your actions, but doing so will only further erode trust and delay the healing process.

Taking responsibility also means being willing to answer your partner's questions about the affair honestly and fully, even when it's uncomfortable or painful. It means being transparent about your whereabouts and actions and following through on your commitments to change. And it means being patient and understanding as your partner works through their own healing process, even when it feels frustrating or unclear.

Remember that taking responsibility is not a one-time event but an ongoing process. It requires consistent effort, self-reflection, and a willingness to hold yourself accountable for your choices and their consequences.

Unpacking the Why

Lonny's Story

When Lonny's wife, Emily, discovered the affair, Lonny struggled to understand his own motivations. He had always considered himself a loyal and devoted partner, and realizing he was capable of such a betrayal was deeply unsettling. In the weeks following the discovery, Lonny grappled with feelings of confusion, shame, and self-doubt. He didn't know if he could control himself.

As Lonny began to work with a therapist, he started to unpack the underlying issues and unmet needs that had contributed to his decision to cheat. He realized he had been feeling disconnected and unfulfilled in his marriage for years but had never communicated those feelings to Emily. He had turned to the affair as a way to escape his own discomfort and dissatisfaction rather than addressing the issues head-on.

Through therapy, Lonny began to understand that his infidelity was not about a lack of love for Emily but about his own struggles with intimacy, communication, and self-worth. He did not feel worthy of Emily's love and devotion. He realized that his father had cheated on his mother, and now he had followed his father's pattern, which he hated. He learned to identify the patterns and triggers that had led him to make such a destructive choice and started to develop healthier coping mechanisms and communication skills.

The Lessons

Unpacking the underlying issues and motivations that led to the affair is crucial in the healing process. It's not about justifying or excusing the behavior but about understanding the factors contributing to the choice to cheat, including relationship patterns.

Some common underlying issues that can contribute to infidelity include:

- Unmet emotional or physical needs in the primary relationship
- Poor communication skills or a fear of conflict
- Unresolved past traumas or attachment wounds
- Low self-esteem or a need for external validation
- Struggles with intimacy or vulnerability
- Untreated mental health issues such as depression or addiction
-Family history of infidelity or relationship issues

By exploring these underlying factors with curiosity and honesty, you can begin to develop greater self-awareness and insight into your patterns and triggers. You can also start to take responsibility for your emotional well-being and learn healthier ways of coping with discomfort or dissatisfaction in your relationship.

It's important to approach this exploration with a non-judgmental and compassionate stance. The goal is not to shame or berate yourself but to understand and take responsibility for your choices so that you can make different ones in the future.

Cultivating Empathy

David's Story

When David's affair was first discovered, he struggled to understand the depth of his wife Rachel's pain. He knew what he had done was wrong, but he couldn't grasp why Rachel was so devastated. He found himself getting defensive when she expressed her anger and frustration, and he struggled to be present with her in her grief. Anytime she began sharing her pain, he felt overwhelmed and uncomfortable. Rather than face this discomfort, he found some subject to argue about.

As David began working on himself in therapy, he developed a deeper sense of empathy for Rachel's experience. He learned to put himself in her shoes and to imagine what it must have felt like to discover the betrayal. He practiced active listening. It took him some time to listen to her pain without changing topics. He also learned to resist the urge to defend or explain away his actions. He also started to understand that rebuilding trust would require consistent effort and patience on his part. Instead of running away, he needed to turn to her.

Through this process, David began to see Rachel's pain not as an inconvenience or obstacle but as a natural and valid response to the trauma he had caused. He learned to sit with her in her grief and to offer support and understanding, even when it was difficult or uncomfortable. He started to see that cultivating empathy was not just about repairing the relationship but about becoming a more caring and compassionate partner overall.

The Lessons

Developing empathy for your partner's experience is essential to the healing process. It's about being willing to see the situation through their eyes and to validate their feelings, even when they are difficult or painful to hear.

Some ways to cultivate empathy include:

- Practicing active listening and resisting the urge to defend or explain away your actions

-Practicing being with your partner in their pain rather than running away from it

- Putting yourself in your partner's shoes and imagining how you would feel in their situation

- Acknowledging and validating your partner's feelings, even if you don't fully understand them

- Being patient and understanding as your partner works through their own healing process

- Educating yourself about the impact of betrayal trauma and the common experiences of betrayed partners

Cultivating empathy requires a willingness to sit with discomfort and prioritize your partner's needs and feelings over your own desire for comfort or forgiveness. It means being present and engaged, even when the conversations are difficult or painful. And it means being willing to do the hard work of rebuilding trust and connection, even when progress feels slow or uncertain.

Remember that empathy is not about taking on your partner's pain as your own but about holding space for their experience with compassion and understanding. By approaching the healing process with empathy and patience, you can create a foundation of safety and trust that can ultimately lead to deeper intimacy and connection.

Making Amends

Sarah and Tom's Story

When Sarah's affair came to light, she knew that she had to take action to repair the damage she had done to her marriage. She started by writing a heartfelt letter to her husband, Tom, expressing her remorse and taking full responsibility for her actions. She acknowledged the pain she had caused and committed to doing whatever it took to rebuild trust and make amends.

In the months that followed, Sarah worked hard to fulfill her commitments. She was transparent about her whereabouts and actions, and she checked in with Tom regularly to see how he was doing. She attended individual and couples therapy, and she made a sincere effort to understand and address the underlying issues that had contributed to the affair.

As time passed, Sarah began seeing small signs of progress in their relationship. Tom started to open up more about his own feelings and needs, and they were able to have more honest and vulnerable conversations. They started to rebuild their intimacy and connection, both emotionally and physically. And while there were still moments of pain and uncertainty, Sarah could see that her consistent efforts to make amends were slowly but surely making a difference. Although she made an initial confession, the ongoing healing required making amends over and over.

The Lessons

Making amends is about taking concrete actions to repair the damage caused by the affair and to demonstrate your commitment to change. It's not just about saying "I'm sorry," but showing through your behavior that you are willing to do the hard work of rebuilding trust and connection. Your spouse may need you to do this several times. It is not that they did not hear or believe you the first time. They need the repetition for things to sink in.

Some ways to make amends include:

- Being transparent about your whereabouts and actions and following through on your commitments

- Attending individual and/or couples therapy to address the underlying issues and develop healthier communication and coping skills

- Making a sincere effort to understand and address your partner's needs and concerns

- Being patient and understanding as your partner works through their own healing process. Give them the time they need to heal.

- Taking concrete steps to prioritize the relationship and to show your partner that they are valued and important to you

Making amends is not a one-time event but an ongoing process that requires consistency, effort, and patience. It's about rebuilding trust through small, daily actions and choices and being willing to show up for your partner even when it's difficult or uncomfortable.

Remember that making amends is not about earning forgiveness or erasing the past but about taking responsibility for your actions and doing the hard work of creating a healthier, more honest relationship moving forward. By approaching the process with sincerity, humility, and a willingness to change, you can begin to lay the foundation for a stronger, more resilient connection with your partner.

The Road Ahead

If you are an unfaithful partner, the road to healing may feel long and uncertain. You may be grappling with feelings of guilt, shame, and confusion, and you may be unsure of how to begin repairing the damage your actions have caused. But by taking responsibility for your choices, unpacking your underlying motivations, cultivating empathy for your partner's experience, and making sincere amends, you can start to lay the foundation for a healthier, more honest relationship.

Remember that healing is a process. There will be setbacks and challenges along the way, and progress may sometimes feel slow or uneven. But by approaching the work with humility, patience, and a willingness to change, you can begin to rebuild trust and create a stronger, more resilient connection with your partner.

It's also important to prioritize self-care and personal growth during this process. Seek the support of a therapist, counselor, church, or support group to help you navigate the complex emotions and challenges of the healing journey. And remember to be patient and compassionate with yourself, even as you work to take responsibility for your actions and their consequences.

Ultimately, the path to healing after infidelity is a deeply personal and individual one. There is no one-size-fits-all approach or timeline for recovery. But by committing to the hard work of self-reflection, accountability, and growth, you can begin to create a new chapter in your relationship - one based on honesty, empathy, and genuine connection.

Reflection Questions:

1. What has been the hardest part of taking responsibility for your actions and their consequences? What support or resources do you need to help you navigate this process with honesty and humility?

2. What underlying issues or unmet needs do you think may have contributed to your decision to engage in infidelity? How can you begin to address these issues healthily and productively?

3. In what ways can you practice empathy and understanding for your partner's experience of betrayal? What concrete actions can you take to demonstrate your commitment to rebuilding trust and connection?

Chapter Seven

The Role of Individual Therapy and Support Groups

When you're in the midst of the pain and chaos of infidelity, it can be easy to feel isolated and alone. You may feel like no one understands what you're going through, or you must bear the weight of your emotions alone. But the truth is, you don't have to navigate this challenging journey alone. Seeking the support of a qualified therapist or joining a support group can be a powerful way to facilitate your healing and growth and connect with others who understand your experience.

The Power of Individual Therapy

Karen's Story

When Karen first discovered her husband's affair, she felt like her entire world had been turned upside down. She was consumed by feelings of anger, betrayal, and self-doubt, and she wasn't sure how to even begin handling emotions that threatened to overwhelm her. At the suggestion of a close friend, Karen decided to seek out the support of a therapist who specialized in infidelity recovery.

At first, Karen hesitated to open up to a stranger about something so personal and painful. But as she began to work with her therapist, she found that having a safe, nonjudgmental space to process her emotions was incredibly helpful. It felt safe to talk about what she was going through and actually being listened to. Her therapist helped her understand that her reactions to the betrayal were normal and valid and that she wasn't alone in her struggles.

Through therapy, Karen began to develop a deeper understanding of her relationship patterns and behaviors. She explored how her family history and past experiences had shaped her beliefs about love, trust, and intimacy and how relationships are done. She started to identify the steps she needed to take to rebuild her sense of self and create a more fulfilling life, with or without her husband.

As Karen continued to work on relationships with her therapist, she found that she could approach the challenges of healing with greater clarity, self-compassion, and resilience. She learned to set boundaries in her relationships, communicate her needs more effectively, and prioritize her own well-being. And while the road to recovery was not easy, Karen found that having the support and guidance of a skilled therapist made all the difference.

The Lessons

Individual therapy can be a powerful tool for facilitating personal growth and healing after infidelity. A skilled therapist can provide a safe, supportive space to process the complex emotions that arise in the aftermath of betrayal and can offer guidance and tools for navigating the challenges of recovery.

Some of the ways that individual therapy can support the healing process include:

- Providing a non-judgmental, empathetic space to process emotions and experiences related to the betrayal

- Helping to identify and challenge negative thought patterns or beliefs that may be hindering healing

- Teaching coping skills and strategies for managing difficult emotions and triggers

- Exploring past experiences or family dynamics that may be influencing current patterns and behaviors in relationships

- Providing guidance and support for setting boundaries, communicating needs, and rebuilding a sense of self and self-worth

It's important to find a therapist who is experienced in working with couples affected by infidelity and whom you feel comfortable and safe with. Look for a nonjudgmental, empathetic therapist with a style and approach that resonates with you. Don't be afraid to shop around or ask for referrals from trusted friends or family members.

There will be setbacks and challenges along the way, but with commitment and effort, individual therapy can be a powerful tool for facilitating personal growth, healing, and transformation.

The Benefits of Support Groups

Melissa's Story

When Melissa's boyfriend admitted to having an affair with his ex-girl-friend, she felt like she had been punched in the gut. She was consumed by feelings of betrayal, anger, and sadness, and she wasn't sure how she was going to move forward. At the suggestion of her therapist, Melissa decided to join a support group for individuals who had experienced infidelity.

At first, Melissa was nervous about sharing her story with a group of strangers. She trusted her therapist, but she didn't know these people. However, as she listened to the other members share their experiences, she felt a sense of connection and validation. She realized that she wasn't alone in her struggles and that there was power in sharing her journey with others who understood what she was going through.

Through the support group, Melissa learned new coping strategies and tools for managing her emotions. She no longer felt alone or like she was the only one this had ever happened to. She received feedback and encouragement from other members, and she found that sharing her own story and offering support to others was incredibly healing. She also formed close bonds with some of the other members and found that having a network of supportive friends who understood her experience was invaluable.

As Melissa continued to attend the support group, she found that she could approach the challenges of healing with greater resilience and self-compassion. She learned to trust herself and her instincts and to set healthy boundaries in her relationships. While the pain of the betrayal never fully went away, Melissa found that the support and connection she experienced in the group helped her move forward with greater strength and clarity.

The Lessons

Joining a support group can be a powerful way to connect with others who understand the pain and challenges of infidelity. You can find validation, encouragement, and practical tools for navigating the healing process in a support group.

Some of the benefits of joining a support group include:

- Connecting with others who have experienced similar challenges and can offer empathy, understanding, and support. This also provides you with someone you can call who is not family or a neighbor.

- Receiving practical advice and guidance from others who have navigated the healing process

- Having a safe space to share your own story and experiences and to process your emotions with others who understand

- Forming close bonds and friendships with other members and building a network of support outside of the group

- Experiencing the healing power of giving and receiving support and witnessing others' growth and progress

When looking for a support group, it's important to find one that feels safe, supportive, and nonjudgmental. Look for a group facilitated by a skilled therapist or counselor that clearly focuses on healing and growth. Don't be afraid to try out a few different groups until you find one that feels like a good fit for you.

Joining a support group is a sign of strength and courage. By reaching out for support and connection, you are taking an active step towards your own healing and growth.

Addressing Personal Issues and Patterns

Tom's Story

When Tom's wife revealed that she had been having an affair with a coworker, he was devastated. He had always prided himself on being a good husband and father, and he couldn't understand how his wife could have betrayed him in such a way. As he began to work with a therapist in the aftermath of the revelation, however, Tom started to realize that there were deeper issues and patterns in his own life that had contributed to the challenges in his marriage.

Through therapy, Tom began to explore his family history and how his early experiences had shaped his beliefs about relationships and intimacy. He realized that he tended to avoid conflict and suppress his own needs and emotions to keep the peace. He also recognized that he had a deep-seated fear of abandonment, which led him to cling to his wife and avoid confronting issues in their relationship.

As Tom continued to work with his therapist, he began to develop greater self-awareness and to take responsibility for his own role in the challenges of his marriage. He learned new communication skills and strategies for expressing his needs and emotions in a healthy manner. He also worked on building a stronger sense of self and developing his own interests and hobbies outside of his relationship.

Through this self-discovery and personal growth process, Tom found that he could approach the challenges of healing from the affair with greater resilience and clarity. He was able to have more honest and open conversations with his wife and to work towards rebuilding trust and intimacy in their relationship. While the process was not always easy, Tom found that by addressing his own personal issues and patterns, he was able to create a stronger, more fulfilling life for himself and his family

The Lessons

While the immediate focus after infidelity is often on the relationship itself, it's important to also take time to explore and address personal issues and patterns that may be contributing to the relationship's challenges. By understanding our histories, beliefs, and behaviors, we can develop greater self-awareness and take steps toward personal growth and healing.

Some common personal issues and patterns that may contribute to relationship challenges include:

- Unresolved childhood wounds or traumas that impact our ability to trust or be vulnerable in relationships

- Difficulty communicating needs and emotions in a healthy way

- Tendencies towards codependency or people-pleasing

- Fear of abandonment or rejection that leads to clingy or controlling behaviors

- Difficulty setting boundaries or asserting oneself in relationships

By working with a skilled therapist or counselor, individuals can begin to identify and address these personal issues and patterns and develop new skills and strategies for creating healthier, more fulfilling relationships.

It's important to approach this process with compassion and patience and to remember that personal growth is a lifelong journey. There may be setbacks and challenges along the way, but by committing to the work of self-discovery and healing, we can create a stronger, more resilient foundation for ourselves and our relationships.

The Path Forward

Healing from infidelity is a complex and deeply personal journey, one that requires courage, compassion, and a willingness to face difficult truths and emotions. While the path forward may feel daunting at times, know that you don't have to navigate this journey alone. By seeking the support of a skilled therapist or counselor, joining a support group, or exploring your issues and patterns, you can take active steps toward healing and growth.

Setbacks and challenges are a normal part of the recovery journey. Be gentle with yourself and with your partner, and trust that with time, effort, and support, you can emerge from this difficult chapter stronger, wiser, and more resilient than before.

Reflection Questions:

1. What fears or hesitations do you have about seeking the support of a therapist or joining a support group? What steps can you take to address these concerns and prioritize your own healing and growth?

2. In what ways have your own personal history, beliefs, or patterns impacted your relationship? What insights or realizations have you had about your own role in the challenges you're facing?

3. What kind of support or guidance do you feel would be most helpful to you in your healing journey? What qualities or characteristics are you seeking in a therapist or support group?

Part III: Healing as a Couple

Restore The Family Press

Chapter Eight

The Importance of Open and Honest Communication

In the aftermath of infidelity, it can be tempting for couples to sweep the painful emotions and difficult conversations under the rug. The betrayed partner may feel too hurt or angry to talk openly, while the unfaithful partner may be consumed by guilt, shame, or defensiveness. But as challenging as it may be, honest and vulnerable communication is essential for any couple hoping to heal and rebuild their relationship after an affair. They each need to share from the heart without attacking each other while they are vulnerable.

Creating a Safe Space

Cindy and Jack's Story

When Cindy first discovered Jack's affair, she felt like her world had been shattered. She was consumed by a whirlwind of painful emotions - anger, betrayal, sadness, and confusion - and the thought of talking to Jack about what had happened felt overwhelming and even frightening. Jack, too, was struggling with his complex feelings of guilt, shame, and uncertainty about the future of their relationship.

In the early days and weeks after the revelation, Cindy and Jack's attempts at communication often devolved into heated arguments or painful silences. They both felt like they were walking on eggshells, afraid to say the wrong thing or to accidentally trigger a fresh wave of hurt or anger in the other.

It wasn't until they began working with a couples therapist that Emily and Jack started to learn how to create a safe space for vulnerable conversations. Their therapist helped them to establish ground rules for their discussions, such as avoiding blame and criticism, taking turns speaking and listening rather than talking over each other, and respecting each other's emotional boundaries.

At first, these structured conversations felt awkward and unnatural. However, as Cindy and Jack continued to practice, they began to find a new level of emotional intimacy and connection. They learned to express their feelings and needs without attacking or shutting down and to listen to each other with empathy and validation. It took several tries, but they finally changed their old habits of handling differences. Slowly but surely, they began to rebuild a foundation of trust and understanding, one vulnerable conversation at a time.

The Lesson

Creating a safe space for open and honest communication is essential for any couple working to heal from infidelity. When emotions are running high, and trust has been broken, conversations can all too easily escalate into conflict or shut down entirely. By establishing clear guidelines and boundaries for your discussions, you can create a container for the difficult emotions and topics that must be addressed.

Some key elements of creating a safe space for communication include:

- Choosing a neutral, private location where you both feel comfortable and free from distractions. At first, you may need to make sure there is a table between you.

- Setting aside dedicated time for your conversations and committing to staying present and engaged even when it feels uncomfortable

- Agree on ground rules for your discussions, such as avoiding blame, criticism, or defensiveness and taking breaks when emotions become overwhelming. You may need to stop the conversation when either of you stands up.

- Respecting each other's emotional boundaries and need for space or time-outs when necessary

- Approaching the conversation with a spirit of curiosity, empathy, and a willingness to listen and understand each other's perspectives

Creating a safe space for communication is an ongoing process. It requires patience, practice, and a commitment from both partners to prioritize emotional safety and connection. But by laying this foundation of trust and openness, you can begin to have the vulnerable, healing conversations that are necessary for moving forward.

The Art of Active Listening

Janet and David's Story

When Janet and David first began couples therapy in the aftermath of David's affair, they both struggled with feeling heard and understood by each other. Janet felt like David was always on the defensive, quick to explain away his actions or minimize her pain. David, in turn, felt like Janet was constantly attacking him, rehashing the past and refusing to see his remorse or efforts to change.

Their therapist introduced them to active listening - a communication technique that fully focuses on and seeks to understand the speaker's message without judgment or interruption. She encouraged Janet and David to take turns sharing their thoughts and feelings while the other practiced listening with curiosity and empathy.

At first, active listening felt unnatural and frustrating for Janet and David. They were so used to jumping in with their opinions or defenses that it was hard to simply listen to the other person's words and emotions. But as they continued to practice, they noticed a shift in their conversations.

When Janet shared her pain and anger about the affair, David learned to resist the urge to explain or defend himself and instead focused on understanding and validating her experience. He did not like to see Janet in pain. It took several times, but he reflected back on what he was hearing, using phrases like "It sounds like you're feeling really betrayed and hurt right now by what I did" or "I can understand why that would be so painful for you."

Similarly, when David shared his own struggles with guilt and shame, Janet practiced listening with compassion and curiosity rather than judgment or blame. It took a while to set aside her anger and desire to hurt him back. She pushed those feelings aside and tried a new way. She asked questions to better understand his perspective, such as "Can you tell me more about what was going on for you at that time?" or "What do you need from me right now to feel supported?"

As Janet and David continued to practice active listening, they found that their conversations became less combative and more collaborative. They were able to have deeper, more vulnerable discussions about the root issues in their relationship and work together towards healing and growth. While the pain of the affair was still present, they felt more equipped to navigate it together with empathy and understanding.

The Lessons

Active listening is a powerful tool for any couple working to improve their communication and connection, but it can be especially vital in the aftermath of infidelity. When emotions are raw and trust has been broken, it can be too easy to fall into old patterns of blame, defensiveness, or disengagement. By practicing active listening, couples can create a space for both partners to feel heard, understood, and validated.

Some key elements of active listening include:

- Giving your full attention to your partner when they are speaking, without interrupting or mentally preparing your response. If you ask questions, limit them to clarifying what was said

- Showing interest and engagement through your body language, such as maintaining eye contact, nodding, or leaning in

- Reflecting back on what your partner says, using phrases like "What I'm hearing is..." or "It sounds like you're feeling..."

- Ask open-ended questions to understand better your partner's perspective or experience, such as "Can you tell me more about that?" or "What was that like for you?"

- Resisting the urge to judge, blame, or defend yourself and instead focusing on understanding and empathizing with your partner's experience

Active listening can feel awkward or challenging at first, especially if you're used to more reactive or defensive communication patterns. But with practice and patience, it can become a powerful tool for deepening intimacy, building trust, and fostering healing in your relationship.

Expressing Needs and Feelings

Kevin and Renee's Story

In the early stages of their healing process after Renee's affair, Kevin struggled to express his own needs and feelings in their conversations. He was so focused on understanding Renee's perspective and avoiding further conflict that he often neglected his emotions and desires. As a result, he found himself feeling increasingly resentful and disconnected from Renee.

With the help of their therapist, Kevin began to learn the importance of expressing his own needs and feelings in a clear, non-blaming way. He practiced using "I" statements, such as "I feel hurt and betrayed when I think about the affair" or "I need some reassurance from you that you're committed to our relationship."

At first, Kevin worried that expressing his needs would appear selfish or demanding. However, as he continued to practice, he found that owning his emotions and desires helped to create more clarity and connection in their conversations. By sharing his vulnerabilities and needs, he invited Renee to do the same, fostering a deeper level of intimacy and understanding between them.

Renee also learned to express her needs and feelings without blame or defensiveness. She practiced taking responsibility for her emotions, using phrases like "I feel ashamed and regretful about my actions" or "I need your support and patience as I work to rebuild your trust." By owning her own experience and needs, she helped to create a more equitable and compassionate dynamic in their relationship.

As Kevin and Renee continued to practice expressing their needs and feelings, they found that their conversations became more authentic and meaningful. They were able to have tough discussions about the affair and its impact without getting stuck in cycles of blame or avoidance. And they began to build a new level of emotional intimacy and trust rooted in a deep understanding and appreciation of each other's inner worlds.

The Lessons

Expressing your own needs and feelings is a crucial skill for any healthy relationship, but it can be especially important after infidelity. When trust has been broken, and emotions are running high, focusing solely on the other person's actions, reactions, or feelings can be tempting, neglecting your inner experience. But by learning to own and express your emotions and desires in a clear, non-blaming way, you can foster a deeper level of intimacy and understanding in your relationship.

Some key elements of expressing needs and feelings include:

- Use "I" statements to own your emotions and experiences rather than blaming or accusing your partner

- Being specific and clear about what you're feeling and what you need, rather than expecting your partner to read your mind

- Taking responsibility for your own emotions and needs rather than making your partner responsible for your happiness or well-being

- Expressing your needs and feelings in a calm, non-judgmental way, even when the topic is difficult or uncomfortable

- Being open to hearing and validating your partner's needs and feelings in return, even if they differ from your own

Learning to express your needs and feelings can be a vulnerable and challenging process, especially if you're not used to prioritizing your own emotions or desires. But by practicing this skill with patience and compassion, you can create a more authentic and intimate connection with your partner, built on a foundation of mutual understanding and respect.

The Road Ahead

Open and honest communication is the lifeblood of any healthy relationship, but it can be especially vital in the aftermath of infidelity. When trust has been shattered and emotions are running high, it can be too easy for couples to shut down, lash out, or avoid difficult conversations altogether. But by committing to creating a safe space for vulnerable dialogue, practicing active listening and validation, and expressing your own needs and feelings with clarity and compassion, you can begin to rebuild the intimacy and connection that has been lost. Healing only happens when both of you feel safe.

Communication that heals is a skill that takes practice and patience to develop. Along the way, there will be moments of discomfort, frustration, or even conflict. But by approaching these challenges with a spirit of curiosity, empathy, and a willingness to grow, you can use even the most difficult conversations as opportunities for deeper understanding and closeness.

As you continue your healing journey, prioritize open and honest communication as a daily practice and a core value in your relationship. Create regular time and space for vulnerable conversations, and commit to showing up with your whole heart, even when it feels scary or uncomfortable. And trust that by doing the hard work of authentic dialogue and connection, you are laying the foundation for a stronger, more resilient bond, one conversation at a time.

Reflection Questions:

1. What are some of the biggest barriers or challenges you face regarding open and honest communication in your relationship? What steps can you take to start to overcome these obstacles?

2. Reflect on a recent conversation with your partner that felt particularly healing or connecting. What made that conversation feel safe and meaningful for you? What can you learn from that experience to bring into future dialogues?

3. What core needs and feelings do you want to prioritize expressing in your conversations with your partner? How can you practice communicating these needs and emotions with clarity, vulnerability, and compassion?

Chapter Nine

Rebuilding Trust and Intimacy

In the aftermath of an affair, one of the most daunting challenges couples face is the task of rebuilding trust and intimacy. The betrayal of infidelity can shatter the relationship's foundation of trust, leaving both partners feeling vulnerable, hurt, and disconnected. But while the road to recovery may be long and difficult, it is possible to heal the wounds of betrayal and create an even stronger, more resilient bond. In this chapter, we'll explore the key elements of the trust-building process, the importance of transparency and accountability, and the role of forgiveness in healing.

The Trust-Building Process

Beth and Daniel's Story

When Beth first discovered Daniel's affair, she felt like the very ground beneath her feet had crumbled. The man she had trusted implicitly, the one she had built a life and family with, had betrayed her in the most intimate way possible. In the following weeks and months, Beth struggled to imagine ever trusting Daniel again. Whenever he came home late or had to take a phone call in another room, she was consumed by fears and suspicions.

Daniel, too, was grappling with the fallout of his actions. He was wracked with guilt and shame over the pain he had caused Beth, and he desperately wanted to prove to her that he could be the faithful, trustworthy partner she deserved. But he often got defensive or frustrated when Beth expressed doubts or asked for reassurance. Daniel believed the affair issue had been discussed at length and was settled.

It wasn't until Beth and Daniel began working with a couples counselor that they started understanding the nature of the trust-building process. Their therapist explained that rebuilding trust was not a one-time event but a journey that would require patience, consistency, and a willingness to step outside their comfort zones.

Together, Beth and Daniel began to work on creating a new foundation of trust in their relationship. They set clear boundaries and expectations around transparency and communication, and Daniel committed to being fully accountable for his actions and whereabouts. He agreed to call when he was running late. They also worked on rebuilding emotional and physical intimacy, starting with small acts of affection and gradually working up to more vulnerable conversations and experiences.

The process was not always easy or clear. There were moments of doubt, fear, and even despair along the way. But as Beth and Daniel continued to show up for each other with honesty, empathy, and a commitment to growth, they began to see glimmers of hope and healing. Slowly but surely, they were able to create a new chapter in their relationship - one built on a foundation of hard-earned trust and resilience.

The Lessons

Rebuilding trust after infidelity is a gradual, often challenging process that requires patience, consistency, and a willingness to step outside of one's comfort zone. Both partners need to have realistic expectations about the trust-building journey's timeline and nature and approach it with a spirit of compassion and understanding.

Some key elements of the trust-building process include:

- Setting clear boundaries and expectations around transparency, communication, and accountability. Some boundaries are non-negotiable, while others are open to negotiation. Be clear whether the boundary is negotiable or not

- Being consistent in one's actions and words and following through on commitments and promises

- Practicing vulnerability and emotional intimacy, even when it feels scary or uncomfortable. This amounts to sharing from your heart, not just from your head.

- Acknowledging and validating each other's feelings and experiences, even when they are difficult or painful or you disagree with them

- Celebrating small victories and moments of connection along the way and maintaining hope and perspective during setbacks or challenges

It's also important to recognize that rebuilding trust is a collaborative effort requiring both partners to fully engage and commit to the process. The unfaithful partner must be willing to take full responsibility for their actions, express genuine remorse, and work hard to earn back their partner's trust through consistent, trustworthy behavior. The betrayed partner, in turn, must be willing to take the risk of extending trust again, to communicate their needs and boundaries clearly, and to work on their healing and growth alongside their partner.

Rebuilding trust is not about returning to the way things were before the affair but about creating something new and different - a relationship built on a foundation of honesty, transparency, and hard-earned wisdom. By approaching the trust-building process with patience, compassion, and a commitment to growth, couples can heal the wounds of betrayal and emerge stronger and more connected than ever before.

Transparency and Accountability

Jessica and Alex's Story

When Jessica first found out about Alex's affair, one of the things that hurt her the most was the secretiveness and deception that surrounded it. She couldn't shake the feeling that she no longer knew the man she had married and that she could never trust him to be honest with her again. When dating, Jessica had several boyfriends cheat on her, and now her husband cheated on her.

Alex, for his part, struggled with the shame and guilt of his actions and often found himself getting defensive or evasive when Jessica asked him questions about his whereabouts or activities. He considered it an invasion of privacy with frequent references to "his business."

As they began couples therapy, their counselor emphasized the importance of transparency and accountability in the trust-building process. She encouraged Alex to be fully honest and forthcoming about his actions and to provide Jessica with any information or reassurance she needed to feel safe and secure in the relationship. This meant giving Jessica access to his phone and email, checking in regularly when he was apart from her, and proactively sharing his thoughts and feelings about the affair and their relationship.

At first, this level of transparency felt uncomfortable and even invasive to Alex. He worried he was losing his privacy and autonomy and that Jessica would use the information against him. He sometimes felt like a child, with Jessica being a controlling mother. But as he continued to practice openness and honesty, he began to see the benefits of their relationship. By being fully transparent and accountable, he demonstrated his commitment to change and rebuilding Jessica's trust. By creating a culture of honesty and openness in their relationship, he and Jessica could have deeper, more authentic conversations and work through the underlying issues that had contributed to the affair.

Over time, Jessica began to feel more secure and trusting in the relationship. She no longer needed to check Alex's phone or question his every move because he had consistently shown her he had nothing to hide. And while the pain of the affair was still present, she felt more hopeful and confident in their ability to move forward together, with honesty and transparency as their guiding principles.

The Lessons

Transparency and accountability are essential components of the trust-building process after infidelity. When trust has been broken, it's crucial for the unfaithful partner to be fully honest and forthcoming about their actions and to take proactive steps to reassure their partner and demonstrate their commitment to change.

Some key aspects of transparency and accountability include:

- Being fully honest and forthcoming about one's actions, thoughts, and feelings, even when it is uncomfortable or difficult

- Providing access to phones, email, and social media accounts, and being willing to check in regularly when apart from one's partner

- Being proactive in sharing information and offering reassurance rather than waiting for one's partner to ask or express concern

- Taking full responsibility for one's actions and their impact on the relationship without defensiveness or blame-shifting

- Consistently following through on commitments and promises and demonstrating trustworthiness through actions, not just words

- Creating a culture of honesty and openness in the relationship, where both partners feel safe to share their thoughts, feelings, and needs without fear of judgment or retaliation

It's important to note that transparency and accountability are not about giving up one's privacy or autonomy but creating a new level of openness and trust in the relationship. By being fully transparent and accountable, the unfaithful partner can demonstrate their commitment to healing and growth and can create a foundation for deeper intimacy and connection with their partner.

Of course, transparency and accountability are not a one-way street - both partners must be willing to practice honesty and openness in the relationship. The betrayed partner, too, must be willing to communicate their needs and boundaries clearly and to extend trust and forgiveness as their partner demonstrates their trustworthiness over time. By working together to create a culture of transparency and accountability, couples can heal the wounds of betrayal and build a stronger, more resilient bond.

Rekindling Intimacy

Mandy and Chris's Story

In the aftermath of Chris's affair, Mandy struggled to feel close or connected to him in any way. The thought of physical intimacy felt impossible, and even emotional intimacy seemed out of reach. She did not want to be physically close to him at all. She was consumed by feelings of betrayal, anger, and self-doubt, and she couldn't imagine ever feeling safe or vulnerable with Chris again.

Chris, too, was struggling with the fallout of his actions. He desperately wanted to reconnect with Mandy and show her how much he loved and valued her, but he didn't know how to bridge the chasm that had grown between them. He often felt rejected and alone, and he worried that the damage to their relationship was irreparable.

As they worked with their therapist, Mandy and Chris began to understand the importance of rekindling intimacy in their relationship. Their therapist explained that intimacy was about more than just physical touch or sex - it was about emotional connection, vulnerability, and trust. He encouraged them to start small, with simple acts of affection and kindness, and to rebuild their emotional bond before jumping back into a physical relationship.

Mandy and Chris began to prioritize spending quality time together without the distractions of work, technology, or outside stressors. They went on walks in the park, cooked meals together, and had long conversations about their hopes, dreams, and fears. They also worked on gradually rebuilding their physical intimacy, starting with holding hands, hugging, and cuddling. They eventually worked up to more intimate acts as they both felt ready and comfortable.

As they continued to prioritize intimacy and connection, Mandy and Chris began to feel a new sense of closeness and understanding. They were able to have deeper, more vulnerable conversations about the affair and its impact and work through the painful emotions and experiences together. While the process was not always easy or comfortable, they both recognized the importance of rekindling intimacy as a key part of their healing journey.

The Lessons

Rekindling intimacy is a crucial aspect of rebuilding a relationship after infidelity. When trust has been broken, and emotions are raw, it can be challenging for couples to feel close or connected in any way. However, by prioritizing emotional and physical intimacy, couples can begin to heal the wounds of betrayal and create a new foundation for their relationship.

Some key aspects of rekindling intimacy include:

- Prioritizing quality time together without distractions or outside stressors

- Focusing on emotional connection and vulnerability through deep conversations, shared activities, and acts of kindness, gratitude, and affection

- Rebuilding physical intimacy gradually, starting with small acts of affection and working up to more intimate experiences as both partners feel ready and comfortable

- Communicating openly and honestly about one's needs, desires, and boundaries around intimacy, and respecting each other's comfort levels and pacing

- Seeking professional support or guidance if intimacy issues persist or feel overwhelming and recognizing that rebuilding intimacy is a process that takes time and patience

It's important to remember that rekindling intimacy is not about trying to recreate the same relationship that existed before the affair but about creating something new and different - a bond built on a foundation of honesty, vulnerability, and hard-earned trust. By approaching intimacy with patience, compassion, and a willingness to step outside one's comfort zone, couples can heal the wounds of betrayal and create a deeper, more authentic connection.

The Role of Forgiveness

Maria and David's Story

For Maria, one of the hardest parts of moving forward after David's affair was the idea of forgiveness. She struggled with the concept of letting go of her anger and pain. She worried that forgiving David would somehow mean condoning his actions or letting him off the hook for the damage he had caused. She also feared that forgiveness would make her vulnerable to future betrayals and that she would never be able to fully trust David again.

As they worked with their therapist, however, Maria began to understand that forgiveness was not about excusing David's behavior or forgetting the pain of the affair but about choosing to release the hold that anger and resentment had on her own life. She learned that forgiveness was a process, not a one-time event and that she needed to do it for herself, not just for David or their relationship.

With the support of their therapist, Maria and David began to work on the process of forgiveness together. David took full responsibility for his actions and expressed genuine remorse for the pain he had caused. He also committed to making amends and rebuilding trust through consistent, trustworthy behavior. Maria, in turn, worked on processing her emotions and experiences and communicating her needs and boundaries clearly to David.

As they continued to work on forgiveness, Maria and David began to feel a new sense of freedom and lightness in their relationship. They were able to have more open, honest conversations about the affair and its impact without getting stuck in cycles of blame or defensiveness. While the pain of the betrayal was still present, they both recognized that forgiveness was a crucial part of their healing journey—not a destination but a daily practice of letting go and moving forward.

The Lessons

Forgiveness is a complex and often misunderstood concept, especially in the context of infidelity. Many betrayed partners struggle with the idea of forgiveness, fearing that it means excusing their partner's behavior or letting them off the hook for the pain they have caused. But in reality, forgiveness is a crucial part of the healing process—not just for the relationship but also for the individual.

Some key aspects of forgiveness include:

- Understanding that forgiveness is a choice and a process, not a one-time event or a feeling

-Couples must forgive each other even if they do not stay married. You forgive the person, not the act

- Recognizing that forgiveness is something you do for yourself, not just for your partner or your relationship

- Letting go of anger, resentment, and the desire for revenge and choosing to focus on your own healing and growth

- Communicating your needs and boundaries clearly to your partner and holding them accountable for their actions and commitments

- Seeking professional support or guidance if forgiveness feels impossible or overwhelming and recognizing that forgiveness is a journey that takes time and patience

Forgiveness does not mean forgetting the pain of the betrayal or excusing the unfaithful partner's behavior. Rather, it is about releasing the hold that anger and resentment have on your own life and choosing to move forward in a healthy and healing way. Forgiveness is also not a one-way street—it requires effort and commitment from both partners to rebuild trust and create a new foundation for the relationship. In most cases, each party needs to forgive.

Ultimately, forgiveness is a crucial part of the healing process after infidelity. By letting go of anger and resentment and working together to rebuild trust and intimacy, couples can create a new chapter in their relationship - one built on honesty, vulnerability, and the strength of their commitment to each other.

The Path Forward

Rebuilding trust and intimacy after infidelity is a challenging and often painful process, but it is possible with patience, commitment, and a willingness to do the hard work of healing. By understanding the nature of the trust-building process, prioritizing transparency and accountability, rekindling emotional and physical intimacy, and practicing forgiveness, couples can create a new foundation for their relationship built on honesty, vulnerability, and resilience.

There will be setbacks and challenges along the way. But by approaching the journey with compassion, patience, and a commitment to growth, you can emerge from the pain of betrayal stronger, wiser, and more deeply connected than ever before.

Reflection Questions:

1. What does rebuilding trust mean to you, and what specific actions or behaviors do you need from your partner to feel safe and secure in the relationship again?

2. How can you prioritize emotional and physical intimacy in your relationship, even when it feels uncomfortable or vulnerable? What small steps can you take to rebuild connection and closeness with your partner?

3. What does forgiveness mean to you in the context of your relationship, and what do you need from your partner (and yourself) to practice forgiveness and let go of anger and resentment?

Chapter Ten

Navigating Triggers, Setbacks, and Conflict

The journey of healing after infidelity is rarely smooth or linear. Even as couples work to rebuild trust, improve communication, and rekindle intimacy, they may face unexpected triggers, setbacks, and conflicts. These challenges can be discouraging and even derailing, leaving both partners feeling frustrated, hopeless, or stuck. But by learning to identify and manage triggers, cope with setbacks, and navigate conflict in a healthy way, couples can build resilience and strengthen their bond, even in the face of adversity.

Although thinking in terms of cause and effect works to solve many problems, it does not work well in relationships. There are patterns at work in relationships where each spouse contributes in some way. Understanding relationships involves looking at the interplay between each spouse.

Identifying and Managing Triggers

Sandra and Bob's Story

Six months after discovering Bob's affair, Sandra felt like she was finally starting to heal and move forward. She and Bob had been working hard in therapy, and she was starting to feel more hopeful and secure in their relationship. But one evening, while watching a movie together, Sandra suddenly became overwhelmed with panic and anger. On the screen, the protagonist had just discovered her partner's infidelity, and the scene felt all too real and familiar to Sandra. In a moment, she felt like she was reliving the moment she discovered Bob's affair.

As the days went on, Sandra started to notice more and more triggers that sent her reeling back into the pain and chaos of the initial discovery. A certain song on the radio, a mention of infidelity in a book or conversation, even the sight of the restaurant where Bob had taken his affair partner - all of these seemingly small things had the power to bring Sandra right back to that horrible moment when she learned of the betrayal.

At first, Sandra tried to push away the triggers and the painful emotions they evoked. She would change the channel, leave the room, or shut down completely, hoping that if she just avoided the reminders, the pain would go away. But as she continued to work with her therapist, Sandra began to understand that triggers were a normal part of the healing process - and that learning to identify and manage them was crucial to her well-being and the health of her relationship.

With the help of her therapist, Sandra began to develop a plan for coping with triggers when they arose. She learned grounding techniques, such as deep breathing and mindfulness, to help her stay present and calm in the moment. She also worked with Bob to create a safe word or signal that she could use when she was feeling triggered so that he could offer support and understanding without judgment or defensiveness.

Over time, Sandra found that while the triggers didn't necessarily go away completely, she could navigate them with greater ease and resilience. She learned to recognize the signs of a trigger coming on and to have compassion for herself and her own healing process. She and Bob were able to use the experience of triggers as an opportunity to deepen their communication, empathy, and understanding of each other's experiences. They discussed them in terms of her reactions and what he said or did that led to them.

The Lessons

Triggers are a common and normal part of the healing process after infidelity. A trigger is any reminder - a thought, sensation, or experience - that brings up painful emotions or memories related to the betrayal. Triggers can be obvious, such as seeing the affair partner or hearing details about the infidelity, or they can be more subtle, such as a certain scent, song, or location that is associated with the betrayal.

When triggers arise, it can feel like all the progress and healing that has been made is suddenly erased, and the pain of the initial discovery is just as raw and overwhelming as ever. However, by learning to identify and manage triggers, couples can build resilience and coping skills to help them navigate these challenges with greater ease and grace.

Some key strategies for managing triggers include:

- Identifying common triggers and developing a plan for coping with them when they arise

- Practicing grounding techniques, such as deep breathing, mindfulness, polyvagal relaxation techniques, or sensory awareness, to stay present and calm in the moment

- Creating a safe word or signal that the betrayed partner can use to communicate when they are feeling triggered and that the unfaithful partner can respond to with support and understanding

- Seeking the support of a therapist or support group to process triggering experiences and develop additional coping strategies

- Practicing self-compassion and recognizing that triggers are a normal part of the healing process, not a sign of failure or weakness

Managing triggers is a skill that develops over time, and setbacks and challenges are a normal part of the journey. By approaching triggers with patience, compassion, and a willingness to learn and grow, couples can use these experiences as opportunities to deepen their bond and build greater resilience and understanding. You are retraining your body, emotions, and brain to create new behaviors and pathways.

Coping with Setbacks and Relapses

Trisha and Chuck's Story

Trisha and Chuck had been working hard to rebuild their relationship after Chuck's affair, and they were starting to feel like they were making real progress. They communicated more openly and honestly and even started to feel some of the old sparks of attraction and intimacy returning. But then, one night, Chuck came home late from work, smelling of alcohol and perfume. Trisha felt like she had been punched in the gut all over again.

As they talked about what had happened, Chuck admitted that he had gone out for drinks with some coworkers, including a woman he had been flirting with at the office. He swore that nothing physical had happened but acknowledged that he had been crossing boundaries and seeking validation outside their relationship.

For Trisha, this setback felt like a huge betrayal of the trust and progress they had been building. She felt angry, hurt, and hopeless, and she wasn't sure if she could ever trust Chuck again. She wondered if all their hard work in therapy had been for nothing and if they were doomed to keep repeating the same painful patterns over and over again.

With the help of their therapist, Trisha and Chuck began to work through the setback and to understand what had led to Chuck's behavior. They explored the underlying issues of insecurity, self-esteem, and unmet needs that had contributed to the flirting and boundary-crossing. They also worked on developing a plan for preventing future setbacks, including setting clear boundaries around opposite-sex friendships and socializing and checking in regularly about any temptations or challenges that arose.

As they continued to work through the setback, Trisha and Chuck began to see it not as a failure or an endpoint but as an opportunity for growth and learning. They could have deeper, more honest conversations about their fears, needs, and desires and develop greater empathy and understanding for each other's experiences. While the setback was painful and challenging, they both recognized that it was an expected part of the healing journey - not a sign that they were doomed to fail, but a reminder of the ongoing work and commitment required to rebuild trust and intimacy.

The Lessons

Setbacks and relapses are a common and normal part of the healing process after infidelity. Even as couples work to rebuild trust and intimacy, there may be moments when old patterns or temptations resurface or when progress feels stalled or even reversed. These setbacks can be discouraging and devastating, leaving both partners feeling hopeless or stuck.

Remember, setbacks are not a sign of failure or a reason to give up on the relationship. Rather, they are opportunities for growth, learning, and deepening understanding. By approaching setbacks with curiosity, compassion, and a willingness to learn and adapt, couples can use these challenges to strengthen their bond and build greater resilience.

Some key strategies for coping with setbacks and relapses include:

- Recognizing that setbacks are an expected part of the healing process, not a sign of failure or weakness

- Exploring the underlying issues and unmet needs that may have contributed to the setback and developing a plan for addressing these issues in a healthy way. This is where a relapse prevention plan is helpful.

- Setting clear boundaries and expectations for behavior and communication moving forward and holding each other accountable to these commitments

- Seeking the support of a therapist or support group to talk about what happened leading to the setback and develop additional coping strategies

- Practicing self-compassion and recognizing that healing is a journey, not a destination, and that progress may not always be linear or straightforward

It's also important to remember that setbacks and relapses do not erase the progress and growth already made. Even in the face of challenges and disappointments, couples can hold onto the moments of connection, understanding, and intimacy they have built together. By approaching setbacks with patience, persistence, and a commitment to growth, couples can emerge stronger, wiser, and more deeply connected than ever before.

Conflict Resolution Strategies

David and Maria's Story

David and Maria had always had a passionate relationship, with plenty of sparks and chemistry. But after David's affair, their passion often turned to conflict, with even small disagreements quickly escalating into heated arguments and bitter accusations. They both felt like they were walking on eggshells around each other, never quite sure what would trigger the next blowup.

As they worked with their therapist, David and Maria began to understand that their conflicts were not just about the specific issues they were arguing about but about the deeper wounds and fears that had been exposed by the infidelity. Maria's anger was rooted in a deep sense of betrayal and loss of trust, while David's defensiveness stemmed from his own shame and guilt over his actions.

With the help of their therapist, David and Maria began to learn new strategies for navigating conflict in a healthy and productive way. They practiced active listening and validation, learning to hear and acknowledge each other's perspectives and emotions without judgment or defensiveness. They also worked on using "I" statements and taking ownership of their own thoughts and feelings rather than blaming or attacking each other.

One of the most powerful tools they learned was the "timeout" strategy. When conflicts escalated and emotions were running high, they agreed to take a break from the conversation and give each other some space to cool down and regroup. They would set a specific time to come back together and resume the discussion, and in the meantime, they would practice self-care and reflection to help them approach the conflict with a clearer and more grounded perspective.

As David and Maria continued to practice these conflict resolution strategies, they began to see a shift in their relationship. While they still had disagreements and challenges, they were able to approach them with greater empathy, patience, and skill. They learned to see conflict not as a threat to their relationship but as an opportunity for growth and deepening understanding. As they navigated these challenges together, they found that their bond was stronger and more resilient than ever before.

The Lessons

Conflict is a normal and inevitable part of any relationship, but in the aftermath of infidelity, it can feel especially intense and high-stakes. When trust has been broken, and emotions are running high, even small disagreements can quickly escalate into painful and destructive fights. However, couples can navigate these challenges with greater skill and resilience by learning and practicing healthy conflict-resolution strategies.

Some key strategies for resolving conflict in a healthy way include:

- Practicing active listening and validation and seeking to understand each other's perspectives and emotions without judgment or defensiveness

- Using "I" statements and taking ownership of one's own thoughts and feelings rather than blaming or attacking the other person

- Setting clear boundaries and expectations for communication and behavior and holding each other accountable to these commitments

- Taking "timeouts" when conflicts escalate, and emotions are running high, and giving each other space to cool down and regroup before resuming the conversation

- Focusing on finding solutions and compromises that work for both partners rather than trying to "win" the argument or prove a point

- Seeking the support of a therapist or mediator to facilitate difficult conversations and provide guidance and tools for healthy communication

Conflict resolution is a skill that takes practice and patience to develop. There may be setbacks and challenges along the way, and progress may not always be linear or straightforward. But by approaching conflict with a spirit of curiosity, compassion, and a willingness to learn and grow, couples can use these challenges as opportunities to deepen their understanding, empathy, and connection with each other.

Ultimately, the goal of conflict resolution is not to eliminate disagreements or challenges altogether but to navigate them in a way that strengthens the relationship and builds greater resilience and trust. By learning to communicate openly and honestly, to validate and support each other's needs and feelings, and to work together towards mutually satisfying solutions, couples can emerge from conflict stronger, wiser, and more deeply connected than ever before.

Navigating triggers, setbacks, and conflict in the aftermath of infidelity can be a daunting and overwhelming task. These challenges can leave couples feeling hopeless, stuck, or tempted to abandon the relationship altogether. But by approaching these challenges with patience, persistence, and a commitment to growth and learning, couples can build the resilience and skills needed to weather any storm.

Setbacks and challenges are normal and expected parts of the process. By learning to identify and manage triggers, cope with setbacks and relapses, and navigate conflict in a healthy and productive way, couples can use these experiences as opportunities for growth, deepening understanding, and strengthening their bond.

It's also important to recognize that healing requires stepping outside one's comfort zone and facing difficult emotions and conversations head-on. This can be scary and uncomfortable at times, but it is through this discomfort that true growth and transformation can occur.

Ultimately, the key to navigating the challenges of healing after infidelity is to approach the journey with patience, compassion, and a commitment to the hard work of growth and change. By supporting each other through the ups and downs, seeking help and guidance when needed, and holding onto hope and faith in the process, couples can emerge from this difficult chapter stronger, wiser, and more deeply connected than ever before.

Reflection Questions:

1. What are some of your most common triggers in the aftermath of infidelity, and how do you typically respond when they arise? What strategies could you try to cope with triggers in a more healthy and grounded way?

2. How have you and your partner navigated setbacks or relapses in your healing journey so far? What have you learned from these experiences, and how can you use this knowledge to build greater resilience and coping skills moving forward?

3. What are your biggest challenges or fears when it comes to navigating conflict in your relationship? What conflict resolution strategies do you think could be most helpful for you and your partner, and how can you practice these skills in your daily life?

Chapter Eleven

Redefining the Relationship

After the initial shock of an affair, you may question everything about your relationship. Can you move past this betrayal? Is it possible to rebuild what's been broken? These are valid questions that every couple must grapple with as they navigate the uncertain terrain of healing.

In this chapter, we'll explore how to assess the viability of your relationship, negotiate a new contract, set goals for the future, and integrate the affair into your shared story. By redefining your relationship intentionally and collaboratively, you can create a stronger, more resilient bond that honors your needs, values, and dreams.

Assessing the Viability of the Relationship

Not every relationship can survive infidelity. Before investing time and energy into reconciliation, assessing whether your relationship has a strong enough foundation to weather the challenges ahead is crucial. Some couples have had enough, and the affair is the final breaking point in their relationship.

Consider the following factors:

1. The nature and duration of the affair

2. The level of remorse and accountability demonstrated by the unfaithful partner

3. The willingness of both partners to engage in the healing process

4. The presence of other issues, such as addiction, abuse, brain damage, or impulse control

Michelle and Robert's decision to stay together after Robert's affair was not easy. They had to look honestly at their 15-year marriage and determine whether they still shared common values, goals, and love for one another. Through couples therapy and individual reflection, they realized that despite the deep hurt caused by the affair, their relationship was worth fighting for.

If you're struggling to assess the viability of your relationship, consider seeking the guidance of a qualified therapist who can help you explore your feelings, needs, and options in a safe, supportive space.

Negotiating a New Relationship Contract

Once you've decided to work on your relationship, it's time to negotiate a new contract—a clear set of agreements and boundaries that will guide your healing journey and lay the foundation for a stronger future together. The old contract of the marriage was violated.

Some key elements to include in your contract:

1. Transparency and accountability measures, such as sharing passwords and allowing access to devices

2. Expectations around communication, intimacy, and quality time together

3. Consequences for breaking agreements or engaging in further betrayal. This also includes a discussion about the violation of the previous contract.

4. Plans for individual and couples therapy

5. A commitment to ongoing check-ins and relationship maintenance

6. A commitment to exclusive monogamy with each other

This contract is not about punishment or control but rather about rebuilding trust and creating a safe, nurturing environment for both partners to heal and grow.

Setting Goals and Creating a Shared Vision

As you redefine your relationship, looking beyond the present moment and envisioning the future you want to create together is important. What kind of partnership do you aspire to have? What dreams and goals do you share?

Take time to discuss your individual and collective aspirations, both short-term and long-term. Some areas to consider:

1. Emotional intimacy and connection

2. Physical intimacy and sexual satisfaction

3. Family planning and parenting (if applicable)

4. Career and financial goals

5. Lifestyle and leisure pursuits

6. Personal growth and spiritual development

By aligning your visions and setting concrete goals, you can work towards a shared sense of purpose and fulfillment that transcends the pain of the affair.

Integrating the Affair into Your Relationship Story

Finally, as you redefine your relationship, it's essential to find a way to integrate the affair into your shared narrative. This doesn't mean glossing over the pain or pretending it didn't happen, but rather acknowledging it as a chapter in your story that you can learn and grow from together.

Some couples find it helpful to create a metaphor or symbolic representation of their healing journey, such as a piece of art, a poem, or a ritual. Others may choose to renew their vows or take a healing trip together to mark this new chapter in their lives.

The key is to find a way to honor your experience and use it as a catalyst for positive change and deepened intimacy. As Nita, a betrayed partner, shared: *"We decided to plant a tree together in our backyard to symbolize our commitment to growth and resilience. Every time I look at that tree, I'm reminded of how far we've come and how much stronger we are now."*

Reflection Questions:

1. What factors do you need to consider in assessing the viability of your relationship? What does your gut tell you about your chances for healing and reconciliation?

2. What would be your non-negotiables if you created a new relationship contract with your partner? What boundaries and agreements feel most important for rebuilding trust and safety?

3. Envision your ideal relationship five years from now. What does it look and feel like? What steps can you take today to start moving towards that vision?

Redefining your relationship after infidelity is a brave and bold act. It requires vulnerability, forgiveness, and a willingness to let go of the past and create something new. By approaching this process with intention, compassion, and a commitment to growth, you can emerge stronger, wiser, and more deeply connected than ever before.

Part IV: Special Considerations

Restore The Family Press

Chapter Twelve

The Impact of Infidelity on Children and Families

When an affair is discovered, the shockwaves reverberate far beyond the couple themselves. Children and extended family members are often caught in the crosshairs, struggling to make sense of the betrayal and navigate their own complex emotions. In this chapter, we'll explore how infidelity affects children of different ages, share strategies for supporting and communicating with them, and discuss how to heal as a family unit.

How Infidelity Affects Children of Different Ages

Children are highly attuned to their family's emotional climate and can sense when something is amiss, even if they don't fully understand it. The impact of infidelity on children varies depending on their age and developmental stage.

Younger children (ages 0-5) may experience:

1. Increased clinginess or separation anxiety

2. Regression in developmental milestones, such as toilet training or language skills

3. Changes in eating or sleeping patterns

4. Increased irritability or emotional outbursts

School-aged children (ages 6-12) may experience:

1. Confusion and anxiety about the stability of the family unit

2. Loyalty conflicts and feeling torn between parents

3. Academic and social difficulties at school

4. Physical symptoms such as headaches or stomachaches

Teenagers (ages 13-18) may experience:

1. Anger, resentment, and a sense of betrayal towards the unfaithful parent

2. Questioning their own beliefs about love, trust, and relationships

3. Acting out through risky behaviors such as substance abuse or promiscuity

4. Difficulty forming healthy romantic relationships in the future

It's important to remember that every child is unique and will process the experience of infidelity differently. Some may appear relatively unscathed, while others may struggle deeply with the aftermath.

Adult Children may experience:

1. Overreact to situations

2. Exhibit intense anger reactions

3. Extreme feelings toward the betrayed parent

4. Abandonment fears

Strategies for Supporting and Communicating with Children

As a parent, your first instinct may be to shield your children from the pain of infidelity. However, trying to keep the affair a secret or minimizing its impact can backfire, leaving children feeling confused, anxious, and alone. Here are some strategies for supporting and communicating with your children during this challenging time:

1. Be honest in an age-appropriate way. You don't need to share all the details but acknowledge that something difficult has happened and that you're working to address it as a family.

2. Reassure them that the affair is not their fault and that both parents still love them unconditionally. Make it clear that they are not responsible for fixing the problem or taking sides.

3. Maintain as much stability and consistency as possible in their daily routines, such as school, extracurricular activities, and family traditions. Children thrive on predictability and structure.

4. Allow them to express their feelings and questions. Listen without judgment and validate their emotional experience. Avoid making promises you can't keep or speaking negatively about the other parent.

5. Seek professional support if needed, such as a child therapist or a support group for children of divorce or infidelity. Having a safe, neutral space to process their emotions can be incredibly helpful.

Remember, your children look to you for guidance and reassurance during this tumultuous time. By modeling resilience, compassion, and a commitment to healing, you can help them weather the storm and emerge stronger on the other side.

Emma's Story:

When Seth and Diane's teenage daughter, Emma, found out about Seth's affair, she was devastated. She lashed out at both parents, saying she could never trust them again. She started skipping school, hanging out with a new crowd, and experimenting with alcohol. Emma did not trust either of her parents.

Recognizing the severity of the situation, Seth and Diane sought the help of a family therapist who specialized in infidelity recovery. Through joint and individual sessions, they learned how to communicate openly and honestly with Emma about what had happened and how they planned to move forward as a family. They realized that Emma was carrying the pain of everyone and, at some level, felt that the affair was her fault. It took a while for her to quit blaming herself.

Though progress was slow and painful at times, Emma gradually began to open up and express her feelings in healthier ways. She learned that it was okay to love both parents while still being hurt and angry about the affair. Over time, with patience and consistent support from her parents and therapist, Emma started to heal and rebuild trust in her family relationships.

Healing as a Family Unit

Infidelity is often described as a "family affair" because it affects everyone in the household, not just the couple. Healing as a family unit requires a collective commitment to honesty, empathy, and forgiveness.

Some steps you can take to facilitate family healing:

1. Engage in family therapy to address the impact of the affair and learn new communication and coping skills.

2. Create positive family interactions and bonding opportunities, such as game nights, movie marathons, or outdoor adventures. Laughter and play can be powerful antidotes to pain and stress.

3. Acknowledge and celebrate each family member's strengths and resilience. Highlight moments of growth, courage, and compassion.

4. Practice forgiveness and letting go of grudges. This doesn't mean forgetting what happened or excusing hurtful behavior but choosing to move forward with an open heart.

5. Embrace new family rituals and traditions that symbolize your commitment to healing and starting fresh. This could be anything from a weekly check-in meeting to an annual family vacation.

There will likely be setbacks and challenges along the way. What matters most is that you approach the journey with patience, compassion, and a willingness to learn and grow together.

Reflection Questions:

1. How have you seen the impact of infidelity on your own children or family members? What have been the most challenging aspects of supporting them through this experience?

2. Reflect on your own childhood experiences with family conflict or betrayal. How have those experiences shaped your beliefs and behaviors in relationships? What kind of family legacy do you want to create going forward?

3. What steps can you take today to prioritize your children's emotional well-being and create a sense of safety and stability in your family? What support or resources do you need to make this happen?

Chapter Thirteen

Infidelity in Blended Families and Second Marriages

Blended families and second marriages come with their own unique set of challenges and dynamics, even without the added complexity of infidelity. When an affair occurs in these contexts, it can be particularly destabilizing, as it threatens not only the couple's relationship but also the delicate ecosystem of stepparents, stepchildren, and ex-partners. In this chapter, we'll explore the specific issues that arise in blended families and second marriages and offer guidance on how to navigate them with grace and resilience.

The Unique Dynamics and Challenges of Blended Families

Blended families are formed when two people with children from previous relationships come together to create a new family unit. While this can be a beautiful opportunity for love, growth, and expanded support systems, it also comes with its fair share of stressors and complications.

Some of the unique dynamics and challenges of blended families include:

1. Loyalty binds and conflicts between biological parents and stepparents

2. Differing parenting styles and expectations

3. Sibling rivalry and competition for attention and resources

4. Navigating complex schedules and living arrangements

5. Integrating extended family members and managing multiple sets of grandparents, aunts, uncles, etc.

When infidelity enters the picture, these pre-existing tensions and fault lines can be exacerbated. Children may feel even more torn between their biological parents or resentful of a stepparent they blame for the affair. Ex-partners may use the betrayal as ammunition in ongoing custody battles or financial disputes. The betrayed partner may question not only their current relationship but also their decision to blend families in the first place.

The extended family may also exert pressure on the blended family. Some members may be loyal to previous family members or disapprove of the current situation.

Scott and Andrea's Story:

Scott and Andrea had both been married before and had children from their previous relationships. When they fell in love and decided to blend their families, they knew it would be challenging but believed their love could conquer all. However, when Andrea discovered that Scott had been having an affair with a coworker, she was devastated on multiple levels.

Not only did she feel betrayed as a wife, but she also worried about how the affair would impact her relationship with Scott's children, who were already struggling to accept her as a stepmother. She feared they would blame her for the breakdown of the marriage and turn against her completely.

Additionally, Andrea's ex-husband used the affair as an opportunity to reopen their custody agreement, arguing that Andrea's home was now an unstable environment for their shared children.

Dealing with Ex-Partners and Stepchildren

One of the most challenging aspects of infidelity in blended families is navigating the relationships with ex-partners and stepchildren. Even in the best of circumstances, these relationships can be fraught with tension, resentment, and competing loyalties. When an affair is thrown into the mix, it can feel like navigating a minefield.

Here are some strategies for dealing with ex-partners and stepchildren in the aftermath of infidelity:

1. Maintain clear boundaries and communication with ex-partners. Avoid oversharing details of the affair or using it as a weapon in ongoing conflicts. Keep the focus on co-parenting and the well-being of the children.

2. Be patient and understanding with stepchildren. Remember that they are processing their own complex emotions and may need time and space to come to terms with the betrayal. Avoid forcing them to take sides or making them feel guilty for their feelings.

3. Seek support from a therapist or counselor who specializes in blended families and infidelity. They can guide you in navigating these tricky dynamics and communicating effectively with all parties involved.

4. Prioritize the safety and stability of the children above all else. This may mean making difficult decisions about living arrangements, custody schedules, or family events to minimize conflict and upheaval.

Building Trust and Stability in a Second Marriage

Infidelity can be particularly devastating in a second marriage, as it may trigger past wounds and fears of abandonment from previous relationships. Couples who have already experienced the pain of divorce or betrayal may feel like they are reliving their worst nightmare all over again.

It is possible to rebuild trust and stability in a second marriage, even after infidelity. The key is to approach the healing process with extra care, patience, and intentionality.

Some tips for building trust and stability in a second marriage:

1. Acknowledge and address any unresolved baggage from previous relationships. This may require individual therapy or counseling to work through past traumas and develop healthier coping mechanisms.

2. Be proactive in creating a strong foundation for your marriage. This may involve attending couples workshops, reading relationship books together, or implementing regular check-ins and date nights.

3. Prioritize open, honest communication and vulnerability. Make space for both partners to express their fears, insecurities, and needs without judgment or defensiveness.

4. Develop a shared vision for your marriage and family life. What kind of relationship do you want to model for your children? What values and priorities do you want to emphasize?

5. Celebrate your unique bond and the love that brought you together. Focus on creating new memories and traditions that honor your commitment to each other and your blended family.

Scott and Andrea's Road to Recovery:

After the initial shock of Scott's affair, Andrea was tempted to throw in the towel on their marriage. She had already been through one painful divorce and couldn't imagine putting herself and her children through that again. However, with the help of a skilled therapist and a lot of hard work, Andrea and Scott slowly began to rebuild their relationship. He was remorseful and took steps to repair their damaged relationship.

They attended a weekend couples retreat where they learned new communication skills and reconnected with their shared values and dreams. They made a point to prioritize date nights and family outings, creating positive memories and experiences to counterbalance the pain of the betrayal. They also worked individually with their children to help them process their emotions and feel secure in the new family dynamic.

It wasn't easy, and there were many setbacks along the way, but Andrea and Scott's commitment to their marriage and their blended family eventually paid off. They emerged from the crisis stronger, wiser, and more deeply connected than ever before.

Reflection Questions:

1. If you are part of a blended family, what unique challenges or dynamics have you faced in your relationships? How might these be impacted by infidelity?

2. Reflect on your communication and co-parenting relationship with any ex-partners. Are there any areas that need improvement or clarification, especially in light of an affair?

3. What specific actions can you take to prioritize the safety, stability, and well-being of any children involved in your blended family during this time of healing?

Chapter Fourteen

Infidelity in Same-Sex Relationships

Infidelity is a painful experience for any couple, regardless of sexual orientation. However, same-sex couples often face unique challenges and pressures when dealing with the aftermath of an affair. From societal stigma and discrimination to a lack of affirming support resources, LGBTQ+ individuals may struggle to find the guidance and understanding they need to heal from betrayal. In this chapter, we'll explore the specific issues that arise in same-sex relationships and offer strategies for navigating the intersection of infidelity and LGBTQ+ identity.

The Unique Pressures and Stereotypes Faced by Same-Sex Couples

Same-sex couples are no strangers to adversity. Despite significant progress in recent years, LGBTQ+ individuals still face discrimination, prejudice, and marginalization in many areas of life. When it comes to relationships, same-sex couples may contend with a range of unique pressures and stereotypes, such as:

1. The myth of lesbian bed death or the assumption that long-term lesbian relationships are sexless and unfulfilling

2. The stereotype of gay men as promiscuous or incapable of monogamy

3. The lack of legal recognition or protection for same-sex relationships in many parts of the world

4. The pressure to be a "perfect" representation of the LGBTQ+ community and prove that same-sex relationships are just as stable and healthy as heterosexual ones

5. The impact of internalized homophobia or shame on relationship dynamics and communication

When infidelity occurs in a same-sex relationship, these pre-existing stressors can compound the pain and complexity of the situation. The betrayed partner may feel like they have not only been wronged by their lover but also by a society that devalues and stigmatizes their relationship. They may fear that the affair will be used as evidence that same-sex relationships are inherently dysfunctional or doomed to fail.

Jenna and Alex's Story:

When Jenna found out that her wife, Alex, had cheated on her with a mutual friend, she was devastated. As a lesbian couple in a small, conservative town, they had always felt like they had to work twice as hard to prove the legitimacy and strength of their relationship. Now, Jenna felt like all their efforts had been for nothing.

She worried about what people would think if they found out about the affair. Would they see it as proof that lesbian relationships were unstable? Would they blame Jenna for not being enough to keep Alex satisfied? Jenna felt a deep sense of shame and isolation as if she had not only failed as a partner but also as a representative of the LGBTQ+ community.

Navigating the Intersection of Infidelity and LGBTQ+ Identity

For many LGBTQ+ individuals, their sexual orientation is a core part of their identity and sense of self. Infidelity can shake their trust in their partner and confidence in their own identity and place in the world.

Some specific challenges that may arise at the intersection of infidelity and LGBTQ+ identity include:

1. Feeling like the affair is a betrayal of the LGBTQ+ community or a rejection of one's identity

2. Struggling to find affirming support resources or therapists who understand the unique dynamics of same-sex relationships

3. Navigating complex dynamics of gender and power in non-heteronormative relationships

4. Dealing with the intersection of infidelity and other marginalized identities, such as being a person of color or having a disability

5. Overcoming internalized shame or homophobia that may be triggered by the betrayal

To navigate these challenges, same-sex couples need to seek out affirming support and resources that validate their experiences and identities. This may involve working with an LGBTQ+-friendly therapist, joining a support group for queer survivors of infidelity, or connecting with other same-sex couples who have weathered similar storms.

It's also crucial for partners to have open, honest conversations about how the affair has impacted their sense of self and identity. This may involve exploring questions like:

- How has the betrayal challenged or changed your understanding of yourself as an LGBTQ+ person?

- What messages or stereotypes about same-sex relationships have been triggered by the infidelity?

- How can you work together to reaffirm your commitment to your identity and your relationship in the face of this crisis?

Finding Affirming Support and Resources

One of the biggest challenges for same-sex couples dealing with infidelity is finding affirming support and resources that understand and validate their unique experiences. While there are many books, websites, and support groups available for heterosexual couples, resources specifically geared towards LGBTQ+ individuals can be harder to come by.

However, they do exist, and seeking them out can make a world of difference in the healing process. Some places to start looking for affirming support include:

1. LGBTQ+-specific therapy directories, such as the ones maintained by the National Queer and Trans Therapists of Color Network or the GLBT National Help Center

2. Online support forums and discussion groups for LGBTQ+ individuals dealing with infidelity, such as the ones on Reddit or Facebook

3. LGBTQ+ community centers or organizations in your area that may offer counseling, workshops, or referrals

4. Books and podcasts that center the experiences of queer and trans people in relationships, such as "The Ethical Slut" by Janet W. Hardy and Dossie Easton or "Multiamory."

5. Affirming religious or spiritual communities that celebrate and support LGBTQ+ love and relationships

You are not alone in this journey, and there is no shame in reaching out for help. Surround yourself with people and resources that celebrate your identity and relationship and remind you of your inherent worth and resilience.

Alex and Jenna's Road to Recovery:

After their initial shock and devastation, Jenna and Alex knew they needed help to navigate the aftermath of Alex's affair. They started by seeking out a couples therapist who specialized in working with LGBTQ+ clients and had experience with infidelity recovery.

In therapy, they were able to explore the unique pressures and stereotypes that had contributed to the breakdown of their relationship. Alex was able to share her struggles with internalized homophobia and the fear that she wasn't "gay enough" because of her attraction to other genders. Jenna was able to express her feelings of betrayal and the worry that the affair would be used to invalidate their relationship and identities.

Together, with the guidance of their therapist, Jenna and Alex began to rebuild trust and intimacy in their relationship. They attended a weekend workshop for same-sex couples healing from infidelity, where they connected with other queer people who understood their struggles. They also found solace in a monthly book club for LGBTQ+ individuals, where they could discuss the intersections of identity, relationships, and personal growth.

Gradually, Jenna and Alex began to see the affair not as a defining moment in their relationship but as an opportunity for greater self-awareness, empathy, and resilience. They emerged from the crisis with a deeper understanding of themselves and each other and a renewed commitment to living authentically and unapologetically as a loving same-sex couple.

Reflection Questions:

1. How might the unique pressures and stereotypes faced by same-sex couples impact the experience of infidelity? What additional challenges or considerations might arise?

2. Reflect on your own journey as an LGBTQ+ person. How has your identity shaped your beliefs and experiences around relationships, trust, and betrayal?

3. What specific support or resources do you need to feel affirmed and validated in your healing journey? Where might you find these resources in your community or online?

Chapter Fifteen

Dealing With Social Stigma and Shame

Infidelity is a deeply personal and emotionally charged experience that can leave individuals feeling isolated, ashamed, and socially stigmatized. The social and cultural attitudes surrounding infidelity often compound the pain and complexity of the healing process, making it difficult for couples to seek support and understanding from others. In this chapter, we will explore the impact of these attitudes, offer strategies for coping with judgment and gossip, and provide guidance on choosing confidants and sharing your story in a way that feels safe and empowering.

Social and Cultural Attitudes Surrounding Infidelity

Infidelity is a topic that evokes strong reactions and opinions from people across all walks of life. In many cultures, cheating is seen as a moral failing, a breach of trust, and a violation of the sacred vows of marriage. These attitudes are often reinforced by religious teachings, media portrayals, and societal norms that prioritize monogamy and fidelity as the ultimate expressions of love and commitment.

As a result, couples dealing with infidelity may face harsh judgment, criticism, and even ostracism from their social circles. The betrayed partner may be seen as a victim or a fool, while the unfaithful partner may be labeled as a liar, a cheater, or a selfish villain. These labels can be incredibly damaging and hurtful, making it difficult for either partner to reach out for help or support.

Moreover, the stigma surrounding infidelity can vary depending on factors such as gender, culture, and social status. In some communities, men who cheat are seen as "players" or "studs," while women who cheat are branded as "sluts" or "homewreckers" or the more creative "slores". These double standards can make it even harder for individuals to process their experiences and seek help without fear of being shamed or blamed.

Lynn and Frank's Story:

Lynn and Frank had been married for ten years when Lynn discovered that Frank had been having an affair with a coworker. Lynn was devastated and felt like her entire world had been turned upside down. To make matters worse, when she confided in her best friend about the situation, her friend's first response was, "Well, what did you expect? Men are just wired differently. Maybe he wouldn't have strayed if you had been more attentive to his needs."

Lynn was shocked and hurt by her friend's reaction. She had been expecting empathy and support, not judgment and blame. The experience left her feeling even more alone and ashamed, as if the affair was somehow her fault.

Strategies for Coping with Judgment and Gossip

When dealing with the fallout of infidelity, it's essential to develop strategies for coping with judgment, gossip, and unsolicited opinions from others. Here are some tips for navigating these challenges:

1. Set clear boundaries with family and friends. Let them know what kind of support you need (and what you don't need) during this time. If someone is being judgmental or hurtful, gently remind them that you seek understanding, not criticism.

2. Practice self-compassion and positive self-talk. Remind yourself that you are not defined by the affair or other people's opinions. You are a worthy, lovable person who deserves respect and kindness, no matter what challenges you face.

3. Seek out supportive communities and resources. Consider joining a support group for individuals or couples dealing with infidelity or working with a therapist who specializes in affair recovery. Surrounding yourself with others who understand your experience can help you feel less alone and more validated.

4. Focus on your healing and growth. Rather than getting caught up in what others are saying or thinking about your situation, turn your attention inward and focus on your own emotional and relational work. Remember that the only opinion that truly matters is your own.

Choosing Who to Confide in and How to Share Your Story

One of the most challenging aspects of dealing with infidelity is deciding who to confide in and how much to share about your experience. While having a support system is important, it's equally important to be selective about who you trust with your story and your vulnerabilities.

Here are some guidelines for choosing confidants and sharing your story:

1. Choose people who have earned your trust and respect. Look for individuals who have demonstrated empathy, discretion, and nonjudgmental listening skills in the past. Avoid people who are known gossipers or who have a history of betraying confidences.

2. Be clear about your boundaries and expectations. Let your confidants know what you need from them in terms of support and what you are and are not comfortable sharing. Make it clear that you seek a safe, nonjudgmental space to process your experiences. Rather than the boundaries being preferences, try writing them down in terms of what you will or will not accept or do.

3. Share your story in stages as you feel ready. You don't have to disclose every detail of the affair or your healing process right away. Share what feels authentic and manageable in the moment, and trust that you can reveal more over time as you build trust and rapport with your confidants.

4. Consider the impact of your story on others. If you have children, extended family members, or mutual friends who may be affected by the news of the affair, be thoughtful about how and when you share your story. In some cases, it may be appropriate to keep certain details private in order to protect the well-being of others.

Lynn and Frank's Road to Recovery:

When Frank and Lynn began the process of healing from Frank's affair, they were initially hesitant to share their story with others, especially after Lynn's best friend's reaction. They feared judgment, gossip, and the possibility of their children finding out about the infidelity.

However, as they worked with their therapist, they realized that they needed additional support and guidance to navigate the challenges of affair recovery. They decided to confide in a trusted couple from their church who had been through a similar experience and had come out stronger on the other side.

The couple provided a safe, nonjudgmental space for Frank and Lynn to share their story and process their emotions. They offered practical advice, empathetic listening, and a reminder that healing was possible, even in the face of such deep betrayal.

Through this experience, Frank and Lynn learned the value of selective, intentional vulnerability. They discovered that by choosing the right confidants and sharing their stories in a way that felt authentic and manageable, they could find the support and validation they needed to move forward in their healing journey.

Reflection Questions:

1. Have you experienced judgment, gossip, or stigma related to infidelity in your own life? How did it impact your healing process and your willingness to seek support?

2. Who do you trust to provide nonjudgmental, empathetic support in your life? What qualities do they possess that make you feel safe and understood?

3. As you consider sharing your story with others, what boundaries and expectations feel important for you to communicate upfront? How can you prioritize your own emotional safety and well-being in the process?

Part V: Moving Forward

Restore The Family Press

Chapter Sixteen

Maintaining Progress and Preventing Relapse

Healing from infidelity is a complex and ongoing process that requires continued effort, commitment, and vigilance from both partners. Even after the initial crisis has passed and the couple has made significant strides in their recovery, it is essential to maintain progress and prevent relapse into old patterns and behaviors. In this chapter, we will explore strategies for continuing the work of healing and growth, nurturing intimacy and connection, identifying and addressing potential risk factors, and creating a culture of transparency and accountability within the relationship.

Continuing the Work of Healing and Growth

Healing from infidelity is a lifelong journey of self-discovery, personal growth, and relationship renewal. To maintain progress and prevent relapse, both partners must continue the work of healing and growth, both individually and as a couple.

Some strategies for continuing this work include:

1. Engaging in ongoing individual therapy to address personal issues, such as low self-esteem, childhood trauma, or attachment wounds, that may have contributed to the infidelity or hindered the healing process.

2. Attending couples therapy on a regular basis to continue building communication skills, working through unresolved conflicts, and deepening emotional intimacy and connection.

3. Participating in workshops, retreats, or support groups focused on affair recovery, personal growth, or relationship enhancement.

4. Reading books, articles, or other resources that provide guidance and inspiration for the healing journey and discussing insights and takeaways with each other.

5. Practicing daily habits and rituals that promote self-care, resilience, and positive relationship dynamics, such as gratitude journaling, mindfulness meditation, or acts of kindness and appreciation towards one another.

Bill and Jeanine's Story:

After the initial crisis of Bill's affair had passed, he and his wife, Jeanine, committed to continuing the work of healing and growth in their relationship. They attended weekly couples therapy sessions, where they practiced new communication skills and worked through the lingering trust issues and emotional wounds from the infidelity.

Jeanine also began individual therapy to address her long-standing struggles with anxiety and self-worth, which had been exacerbated by the betrayal. Through this work, she developed a stronger sense of self and learned to set healthier boundaries in her relationships.

Together, Bill and Jeanine participated in a weekend couples retreat focused on rebuilding intimacy and connection. The retreat provided them with valuable tools and insights for nurturing their bond and creating a shared vision for their future.

By prioritizing their individual and collective growth, Bill and Jeanine maintained their progress and deepened their commitment to a stronger, more resilient relationship.

Nurturing Intimacy and Connection

One of the most significant challenges in the aftermath of infidelity is rebuilding intimacy and connection between partners. The betrayal of trust can create a deep sense of emotional distance and disconnection, making it difficult for couples to feel close and secure in their relationship.

Couples must be intentional about creating opportunities for bonding, vulnerability, and shared experiences to nurture intimacy and connection.

Some strategies for achieving this include:

1. Scheduling regular date nights or quality time together, free from distractions or discussions about the affair.

2. Engaging in shared activities or hobbies that promote teamwork, playfulness, and mutual enjoyment, such as dancing, hiking, or cooking together.

3. Practicing physical touch and affection, such as holding hands, cuddling, or giving each other massages, to promote feelings of closeness and comfort.

4. Sharing hopes, dreams, fears, and vulnerabilities and practicing empathetic listening and validation.

5. Expressing gratitude, appreciation, and admiration for each other's positive qualities and efforts in the healing process.

Liz and Jon's Story:

In the early stages of their recovery, Liz and Jon struggled to reconnect emotionally and physically after Jon's affair. The pain and betrayal had created a deep chasm between them, and they often found themselves retreating into separate corners of the house, avoiding intimate conversations or interactions.

With the guidance of their therapist, Liz and Jon began to prioritize nurturing their intimacy and connection. They scheduled a weekly date night, where they took turns planning fun, engaging activities that allowed them to rediscover their shared interests and enjoy each other's company.

They also committed to daily physical touch, even if it was just a brief hug or a hand on the shoulder. These small gestures helped to rebuild a sense of comfort and safety in their relationship.

Over time, as they continued to practice vulnerability and empathetic communication, Liz and Jon began to feel a renewed sense of closeness and intimacy. They were able to share their deepest hopes and fears and offer each other the support and validation they needed to heal and grow together.

Identifying and Addressing Potential Risk Factors

Preventing relapse in affair recovery requires a proactive approach to identifying and addressing potential risk factors that could threaten the couple's progress and stability. These risk factors can be individual, relational, or environmental in nature and may require ongoing attention and management.

Some common risk factors to be aware of include:

1. Unresolved individual issues, such as mental health problems, addiction, or trauma, that may have contributed to the infidelity or hindered the healing process.

2. Ongoing relationship dynamics, such as power imbalances, poor communication skills, or lack of emotional intimacy, that may create vulnerability to future betrayals.

3. External stressors, such as work/life balance challenges, financial strains, or extended family conflicts, may put additional pressure on the relationship.

4. Risky situations or environments, such as working closely with an attractive colleague, spending time in social settings where infidelity is normalized, or engaging in secretive online behaviors.

To address these risk factors, couples may need to:

1. Seek additional individual or couples therapy to work through unresolved issues or develop coping strategies.

2. Establish clear boundaries and agreements around risky situations or behaviors, such as limiting contact with former affair partners or being transparent about social media use.

3. Develop a shared understanding of each partner's personal triggers and vulnerabilities and create a plan for supporting each other in times of stress or temptation.

4. Regularly assess and adjust their lifestyle, priorities, and support systems to ensure that they are conducive to long-term healing and stability.

Jessica and Mark's Story:

As part of their ongoing recovery work, Jessica and Mark identified several potential risk factors that could threaten their progress. Mark acknowledged that his long-standing pattern of using alcohol to cope with stress and anxiety had likely contributed to his poor decision-making and, ultimately, his affair.

Together, they established clear boundaries around Mark's drinking, such as limiting his alcohol intake and avoiding social situations where heavy drinking was expected. Mark also began attending individual therapy and a support group for professionals struggling with substance abuse.

Jessica recognized that her own tendency to avoid conflict and suppress her emotions had created a climate of disconnection and resentment in their marriage. She committed to working on her assertiveness and emotional expression skills in individual therapy, and the couple began practicing more open, honest communication in their daily interactions.

By proactively identifying and addressing these risk factors, Jessica and Mark were able to create a stronger foundation for their relationship and reduce the likelihood of future relapse.

Creating a Culture of Transparency and Accountability

Preventing relapse in affair recovery requires a fundamental shift in the couple's relationship dynamic from one of secrecy and betrayal to one of transparency and accountability. This shift involves both partners taking responsibility for their actions, being open and honest with each other, and holding each other accountable for maintaining the integrity of their relationship.

Some strategies for creating a culture of transparency and accountability include:

1. Establishing clear agreements around honesty, full disclosure, and information-sharing, such as giving each other access to phones, email accounts, or social media profiles.

2. Regularly checking in with each other about potential temptations, challenges, or concerns and providing support and encouragement for maintaining appropriate boundaries.

3. Taking responsibility for one's own thoughts, feelings, and actions and avoiding blame, defensiveness, or minimization when discussing sensitive topics.

4. Seeking feedback and accountability from trusted friends, family members, or professionals who can guide and support the couple's recovery process.

5. Celebrating successes and milestones in the healing journey and acknowledge each other's efforts and progress in rebuilding trust and intimacy.

Robert and Laura's Story:

After years of secrecy and deception surrounding his multiple affairs, Robert knew that he needed to make a drastic change in his behavior and his relationship with his wife, Laura. With the help of their therapist, Robert and Laura established a new set of agreements and expectations around transparency and accountability.

Robert committed to giving Laura full access to his phone, email, and social media accounts and to informing her of his whereabouts and activities throughout the day. He also began attending individual therapy and a support group for sex addicts, where he could work on his underlying issues and be held accountable for his recovery.

Laura, in turn, committed to being open and honest about her own struggles and needs in the relationship and to providing Robert with clear feedback and boundaries around his behavior. She also began attending a support group for partners of sex addicts, where she could find validation and guidance for her own healing process.

Together, Robert and Laura created a daily check-in ritual, during which they shared their thoughts, feelings, and experiences from the day and offered each other support and encouragement for maintaining their progress. They also celebrated each milestone in their recovery, such as Robert's one-year sobriety anniversary, as a testament to their hard work and commitment to their relationship.

By creating a culture of transparency and accountability, Robert and Laura rebuilt trust, deepened intimacy, and prevented relapse in their ongoing recovery journey.

Reflection Questions:

1. What strategies or practices have been most helpful for you in maintaining progress and preventing relapse in your recovery journey?

2. How have you and your partner worked to nurture intimacy and connection in the aftermath of infidelity? What challenges or successes have you encountered in this process?

3. What potential risk factors do you identify in your own relationship, and what steps can you take to proactively address and manage these factors?

Maintaining progress and preventing relapse in affair recovery requires a comprehensive, proactive approach that addresses individual, relational, and environmental factors. By continuing the work of healing and growth, nurturing intimacy and connection, identifying and addressing potential risk factors, and creating a culture of transparency and accountability, couples can build a stronger, more resilient relationship in the aftermath of infidelity.

Chapter Seventeen

Knowing When to Seek Professional Help

Healing from infidelity is a complex and emotionally challenging process that often requires more than just individual effort and willpower. While some couples may be able to navigate the aftermath of an affair on their own, many others can benefit greatly from seeking professional help and support. In this chapter, we will explore the signs that additional support may be needed, how to find a qualified therapist or counselor, and the benefits of couples therapy and intensive workshops for affair recovery.

The Signs That Additional Support May Be Needed

Recognizing when it's time to seek professional help is not always easy, especially when couples are in the midst of the emotional turmoil and confusion that often follows the discovery of infidelity. However, several key signs can indicate that additional support may be needed to facilitate healing and prevent further damage to the relationship.

Some of these signs include:

1. Persistent feelings of anger, resentment, or bitterness that do not

seem to improve over time, despite individual efforts to work through them.

2. Inability to communicate effectively or have productive conversations about the affair without escalating into conflict or shutting down emotionally.

3. Ongoing trust issues or fears of future betrayal that create significant barriers to intimacy and connection in the relationship.

4. Unresolved individual issues, such as depression, anxiety, or trauma that are exacerbated by the infidelity and interfere with the healing process.

5. A sense of being "stuck" or unable to move forward in the recovery process despite sincere efforts and intentions from both partners.

Melissa and Randy's Story:

Three months after discovering her husband's affair, Melissa found herself struggling to cope with the intense emotions and challenges of the recovery process. Despite her best efforts to forgive and move forward, she couldn't shake the constant feelings of anger, betrayal, and mistrust that consumed her thoughts and interactions with her husband, Randy.

Randy, for his part, was genuinely remorseful and committed to repairing the damage he had caused. However, whenever he tried to express his regret or reassure Melissa, she would either lash out in anger or retreat into a cold, silent distance that left him feeling helpless and disconnected.

As the weeks passed and their attempts at communication continued to deteriorate, Melissa and Randy realized that they needed more than just their own efforts to heal the wounds of infidelity. They decided to seek the guidance of a qualified therapist who could help them navigate the complex emotions and challenges of the recovery process.

How to Find a Qualified Therapist or Counselor

Once a couple has recognized the need for professional help, the next step is to find a qualified therapist or counselor who can provide the necessary support and guidance. However, with so many different types of mental health professionals and approaches to therapy, it can be difficult to know where to start.

Some tips for finding a qualified therapist or counselor include:

1. Seek referrals from trusted sources, such as friends, family members, or healthcare providers who have personal experience with therapy or can vouch for a particular professional's qualifications and effectiveness.

2. Look for therapists or counselors who specialize in couples therapy, infidelity recovery, or other relevant areas of expertise, such as trauma or addiction.

3. Consider the therapist's education, training, and credentials, as well as their approach to therapy and compatibility with your personal values and goals.

4. Schedule an initial consultation or interview with potential therapists to assess their communication style, level of empathy and understanding, and overall "fit" with you and your partner.

5. Don't be afraid to ask questions or express concerns about the therapy process, and trust your instincts if something doesn't feel

right or effective.

Melissa and Randy Find a Therapist:

After recognizing the need for professional help, Melissa and Randy began finding a qualified therapist to support them in their recovery journey. They started by asking their primary care physician for referrals to local mental health professionals who specialized in couples therapy and infidelity recovery.

From there, they researched each therapist's background, approach, and reviews online and narrowed down their list to a few top candidates. They scheduled initial consultations with each therapist, during which they discussed their specific situation, goals, and concerns.

Ultimately, Melissa and Randy chose a therapist who had extensive experience working with couples in the aftermath of infidelity and whose warm, empathetic communication style put them both at ease. They felt confident that this therapist had the necessary skills and expertise to guide them through the challenging work of healing and rebuilding their relationship.

The Benefits of Couples Therapy and Intensive Workshops

Couples therapy and intensive workshops can offer numerous benefits for couples navigating the aftermath of infidelity. These professional interventions provide a safe, structured space for partners to process their emotions, communicate openly and honestly, and develop new skills and strategies for rebuilding trust and intimacy.

Some specific benefits of couples therapy and intensive workshops include:

1. Improved communication and conflict resolution skills can help couples have more productive, less reactive conversations about the affair and its impact on their relationship.

2. Greater insight and understanding into the underlying issues and patterns that may have contributed to the infidelity, such as unmet needs, attachment wounds, or dysfunctional relationship dynamics.

3. Opportunities for guided disclosure and processing of the details and impact of the affair can help couples establish a foundation of honesty and transparency moving forward.

4. Development of a shared vision and plan for the future of the relationship, including specific goals, boundaries, and strategies for preventing future betrayals and maintaining progress.

5. Increased emotional intimacy and connection as couples learn to be more vulnerable, empathetic, and attuned to each other's needs and experiences.

Melissa and Randy's Road to Recovery:

Through their work in couples therapy, Melissa and Randy began to experience significant shifts in their relationship and individual healing. Their therapist helped them establish a safe, non-judgmental space to express their feelings and needs and taught them new communication skills to navigate difficult conversations without escalating into conflict.

They also gained valuable insights into the underlying issues that had contributed to Randy's infidelity, such as his long-standing struggles with low self-esteem and fear of intimacy. With the guidance of their therapist, Randy and Melissa were able to develop a deeper understanding and empathy for each other's experiences and begin the hard work of rebuilding trust and intimacy in their relationship.

In addition to their weekly therapy sessions, Melissa and Randy also attended a weekend intensive workshop for couples recovering from infidelity. The immersive experience provided them with additional tools and strategies for healing, as well as a supportive community of other couples who were navigating similar challenges.

Through the combination of couples therapy and intensive workshops, Melissa and Randy made significant progress in their recovery journey. They developed a stronger, more resilient bond and a shared commitment to ongoing growth and healing in their relationship.

Reflection Questions:

1. What signs or indicators might suggest that you and your partner could benefit from seeking professional help in your recovery journey?

2. How can you find a qualified therapist or counselor who is a good fit for your specific needs and goals as a couple?

3. What specific benefits or outcomes would you hope to achieve through participating in couples therapy or intensive workshops for affair recovery?

Chapter Eighteen

Stories of Courage and Commitment

Navigating the aftermath of infidelity can be a daunting and isolating experience, leaving many couples feeling hopeless and unsure about the future of their relationship. However, it is important to remember that healing and reconciliation are possible and that countless couples have successfully overcome the pain and betrayal of an affair. In this chapter, we will explore real-life examples of couples who have overcome infidelity, the lessons and insights gained from their experiences, and messages of hope and encouragement for those currently on the path to recovery.

Stories of Couples Who Have Overcome Infidelity

While every couple's journey is unique, there is much to be learned from the stories of those who have navigated the challenges of infidelity and emerged stronger and more resilient on the other side. These stories are powerful reminders that healing is possible and that even the most shattered relationships can be rebuilt with commitment, patience, and hard work.

One such couple is Rachel and Marcus, who had been married for 12 years when Marcus disclosed his two-year affair with a coworker. The revelation shook the very foundation of their relationship, leaving Rachel feeling betrayed, angry, and unsure if she could ever trust her husband again.

However, with the help of a skilled couples therapist and a shared commitment to healing, Rachel and Marcus slowly began to rebuild their marriage. They learned to communicate more openly and honestly, to take responsibility for their individual contributions to the breakdown of their relationship, and to prioritize their connection and intimacy daily. They each learned to take responsibility for their own thoughts, emotions, and behavior. The old pattern of Rachel blaming Marcus for her anger or emotional state was changed. She now accepted responsibility for her emotional state without blaming Marcus.

Another couple, Andi and Jenna, faced a similar crisis when Andi discovered Jenna's multiple online affairs. As a same-sex couple already navigating the challenges of societal stigma and discrimination, the betrayal felt like a double blow to their sense of safety and belonging.

Through the support of a compassionate therapist and LGBTQ+ affirming community, Andi and Jenna were able to work through the complex emotions and dynamics of infidelity in the context of their queer identity. They learned to lean on each other and their shared values and to use the crisis as an opportunity for growth and transformation in their relationship.

Lessons and Insights Gained from Their Experiences

While each couple's story is unique, some common themes and insights emerge from the experiences of those who have successfully overcome infidelity. These lessons can serve as valuable guideposts for couples currently navigating the recovery process.

Some of these insights include:

1. Healing is possible but takes time, effort, and patience. There are no shortcuts or quick fixes to the deep wounds of betrayal, but with consistent, intentional work, couples can gradually rebuild trust and intimacy.

2. Both partners must be fully committed to the recovery process. Healing cannot be one-sided but requires both partners' active participation and engagement, even when it is difficult or uncomfortable.

3. Communication is key to rebuilding trust and understanding. Couples must learn to express their thoughts, feelings, and needs openly and honestly, without fear of judgment or retaliation.

4. The affair is often a symptom of deeper issues in the relationship or individual. Addressing these underlying factors, such as unmet needs, attachment wounds, or personal insecurities, is essential for long-term healing and growth.

5. Forgiveness is a process, not a singular event. It involves a daily choice to let go of resentment, to extend empathy and compassion, and to focus on the present and future rather than the past.

Messages of Hope and Encouragement

For couples currently amid the pain and uncertainty of infidelity, it can be difficult to imagine a future where trust and love are restored. However, the stories and insights of those who have successfully navigated this journey offer powerful messages of hope and encouragement.

To those who are struggling, know that you are not alone. The path to healing may be difficult, but it is well-trodden by countless others who have faced similar challenges and emerged stronger and more resilient.

Remember that healing is not a linear process and that setbacks and challenges are a normal part of the journey. Be patient and compassionate with yourselves and each other, and celebrate the small victories and progress along the way.

Trust that the love and commitment that brought you together can be a powerful source of strength and motivation in the face of adversity. Lean on your shared values, dreams, and intentions for your relationship and use them as a guidepost for your recovery.

Above all, hold onto hope. The fact that you are reading this book and seeking support and guidance is a testament to your resilience and determination. With the right tools, resources, and mindset, you, too, can overcome the pain of infidelity and create a new chapter of love, trust, and intimacy in your relationship.

As Rachel, one of the survivors of infidelity mentioned earlier, shared:

"The journey of healing from infidelity is not for the faint of heart. It requires a level of courage, vulnerability, and tenacity that I didn't even know I possessed. But with my husband, our therapist, and our community's love and support, I have discovered a strength and resilience within myself that I never could have imagined. And our marriage, while forever changed, is now deeper, more honest, and more fulfilling than ever before. To anyone currently in the trenches of this journey, you are not alone, and there is hope and healing on the other side."

Reflection Questions:

1. What insights or lessons from the success stories shared in this chapter resonate most with your own experiences or hopes for your relationship?

2. How can you draw upon the examples of resilience and determination these couples demonstrate as you navigate your recovery journey?

3. What messages of hope and encouragement do you need to hear right now to sustain your commitment to healing and growth in your relationship?

Chapter Nineteen

Embracing the Journey of Healing and Growth

As we come to the end of this exploration of healing after infidelity, it is important to take a moment to reflect on the key insights, lessons, and reminders that have emerged throughout this journey. While the path to recovery is rarely easy or straightforward, it is also rich with opportunities for growth, transformation, and renewed love and connection.

The aftermath of an affair can leave you feeling lost, hurt, and unsure of how to move forward. While it may seem daunting, the best way to begin the healing process is to confront the issues head-on. Ignoring the problem or sweeping it under the rug will only prolong the pain and hinder your progress.

Taking the First Steps

Acknowledging the affair's impact and deciding to take action is a crucial first step. By seeking help and resources, you've already begun the process of healing and growth. Remember, you're not alone in this struggle; many couples have successfully navigated this difficult path.

To continue your journey, focus on the following key areas:

- Understanding the lingering effects of an affair and learning how to address them

- Stopping the cycle of hurt and finding closure

- Developing healthy communication skills and reducing conflict

- Prioritizing your relationship and avoiding the use of children as pawns

- Shifting from a reactive mindset to a proactive approach to recovery

A Roadmap to Recovery

Attempting to rebuild your relationship without guidance can feel like planning a complex trip without a map. You might make some progress, but you're likely to encounter many detours and roadblocks along the way.

To ensure you're on the right path, concentrate on these essential elements:

- Restoring intimacy and connection

- Gaining insight into the dynamics of your relationship

- Minimizing the long-term impact of the affair

- Redefining the unwritten rules and expectations of your partnership

- Mastering effective communication techniques

Key Takeaways and Reminders

1. Healing from infidelity is a deeply personal and individualized process. There is no one-size-fits-all approach or timeline for recovery, and what works for one couple may not work for another. Trust your own instincts, needs, and boundaries as you navigate this journey.

2. Communication, honesty, and transparency are essential for rebuilding trust and intimacy. Commit to having open, vulnerable conversations

with your partner and to creating a safe, non-judgmental space for both of you to express your thoughts and feelings.

3. Forgiveness is a choice and a process, not a singular event. It involves a daily decision to let go of resentment, to extend empathy and understanding, and to focus on the present and future rather than the past.

4. Healing requires both individual and collective work. While it is important to focus on your own emotional needs and growth, it is equally crucial to prioritize your relationship and to work together as a team to overcome the challenges of infidelity.

5. Seeking professional help and support is a sign of strength, not weakness. Whether through couples therapy, individual counseling, or support groups, having the guidance and perspective of experienced professionals can be invaluable in navigating the complexities of recovery.

The Possibilities for Post-Traumatic Growth and Transformation

While infidelity is undoubtedly a traumatic and painful experience, it can also be a catalyst for profound growth, self-discovery, and transformation. Many couples who have successfully navigated the journey of healing report experiencing a deeper level of intimacy, authenticity, and resilience in their relationship as a result.

Some of the potential areas for growth and transformation include:

1. Increased self-awareness and personal insight
2. Enhanced communication and conflict-resolution skills
3. Greater emotional and sexual intimacy
4. Stronger boundaries and a sense of personal agency

5. Renewed appreciation and gratitude for one's partner and relationship

6. Expanded capacity for empathy, forgiveness, and compassion

7. A clearer sense of one's values, priorities, and life purpose

By embracing the challenges of recovery as opportunities for learning and growth, couples can emerge from the experience of infidelity stronger, wiser, and more deeply connected than ever before.

Resources for Further Support

If you are currently navigating the aftermath of infidelity, know that you are not alone. While the road ahead may feel daunting, there is hope and support available to guide you through this challenging time.

Some steps you can take to prioritize your healing and well-being include:

1. Reach out to trusted friends, family members, or professionals for support and guidance. You don't have to go through this alone.

2. Regular self-care practices, such as exercise, meditation, journaling, or therapy, can support your emotional and physical health.

3. Educate yourself about the dynamics of infidelity and the recovery process. Read books, attend workshops, or join support groups to gain additional insights and tools for healing.

4. Commit to ongoing, open communication with your partner. Set aside regular time to check in, express your feelings, and work through any challenges or conflicts that arise.

5. Celebrate your progress and milestones along the way. Remember that healing is a journey, and every step forward is a victory worth acknowledging.

Additional resources for support and guidance include:

- Affair Recovery Center (www.affairrecovery.com)

  - Emotionally Focused Therapy (www.iceeft.com)

  - Gottman Institute (www.gottman.com)

  - Marriage Helper (www.marriagehelper.com)

  - National Domestic Violence Hotline (www.thehotline.org)

  - Survive Your Partner's Affair (www.surviveyourpartnersaffair.com)

Your journey is not for the faint of heart. It requires courage, vulnerability, and a willingness to face the pain and uncertainty of a shattered reality. But it is also an invitation to grow, to love more deeply, and to create a new story of resilience and renewal. Healing and recovery are possible. By committing to the work of self-discovery, compassion, and forgiveness and by reaching out for the support and guidance you need, you can emerge from this experience stronger, more resilient, and more deeply connected to yourself and your partner.

May you find the strength, hope, and healing you need to emerge stronger and more radiant than ever before. Remember, you are not alone; there is always hope for a brighter, more loving future.

About The Author

As a teenager, I experienced the devastation caused by infidelity first-hand when my family went through a parental affair. Navigating through the aftermath, which involved children's protective services, domestic abuse, legal fights, and emotional upheaval, left me feeling helpless and alone.

Determined to learn from these experiences, I became a Licensed Professional Counselor (LPC) and Licensed Chemical Dependency Counselor (LCDC). For over 40 years, I have helped thousands of families across various settings, applying an approach founded on proven Biblical principles and neuropsychology discoveries.

As an early pioneer in online counseling, I have been helping people through articles, e-books, and telephone sessions since 1999. My work has been featured on Wall Street Journal Radio, the Larry Elder Show, and numerous other media.

Married since 1985, my wife Peggy and I have been blessed with three incredible sons. We have navigated the challenges and temptations in our own marriage, and I am committed to helping others overcome the pain of affairs and rebuild their relationships.

You may contact me via email at jeff@restorethefamily.com.

Follow me on Medium @RestoreTheFamily

Receive my daily newsletter at www.SurviveYourPartnersAffair.com

The Affair Recovery Workhop

Transform Your Marriage

Are you ready to embark on a transformative journey to heal your marriage and rediscover the love, trust, and intimacy you once shared? The Affair Recovery Workshop, created by renowned relationship expert Jeffrey D. Murrah, LPC, LCDC, is your essential companion to this book, offering a unique and comprehensive approach to navigating the complex emotions and challenges that follow infidelity. With a proven track record of success and a personalized approach tailored to your needs, this workshop provides you with the in-depth guidance, interactive experience, and practical tools necessary to rebuild a stronger, more resilient relationship.

Why the Affair Recovery Workshop is the Essential Companion to this Book

1. In-depth Guidance: While the book lays a solid foundation for understanding infidelity and the recovery process, the video program dives deeper into the critical topics, offering 2.5 hours of expert guidance from Jeffrey D. Murrah. The extended format allows for a more thorough exploration of the strategies and techniques needed to rebuild trust, improve communication, and foster intimacy.

2. Interactive Experience: The video program provides an engaging and interactive learning experience that complements the book. With visual aids, real-life examples, and guided exercises, you can actively apply the concepts and strategies to your own situation, enhancing your understanding and retention of the material.

3. Personalized Approach: The Affair Recovery Workshop recognizes that every couple's situation is unique. The video program offers a personalized approach, helping you identify and address your relationship's specific challenges and dynamics. This targeted guidance can accelerate healing and lead to more effective outcomes.

4. Convenient and Flexible: With 24/7 access to the video modules, a comprehensive 68-page workbook, and a bonus ebook, "How Can I Trust You Again?", you can work through the program at your own pace, from the privacy and comfort of your own home. This flexibility ensures you can fully engage with the content and implement the strategies on your own terms.

Real Testimonials from Transformed Lives

"The Affair Recovery Workshop was the turning point in our healing journey. Jeffrey's in-depth guidance and personalized approach helped us navigate the complex emotions and rebuild our marriage stronger than ever." - Sarah and Michael, married 9 years.

"The interactive experience of the video program, combined with the practical exercises in the workbook, allowed us to dive deeper into understanding and addressing the unique challenges in our relationship. It was a game-changer for us." - Lisa and David, married 14 years.

Your Journey to a Stronger Marriage Starts Here

Invest in your marriage and your future happiness with the **Affair Recovery Workshop**. As a special offer exclusively available through this book, we're extending a 30% discount on the workshop to help you start your transformative journey. Visit **www.AffairRecoveryWorkshop.com** and use the coupon code **WORKSHOP30** to claim your discount. This limited-time offer is our commitment to your success.

Don't let infidelity define your marriage. Take the first step towards healing and renewal today, and give yourself the best opportunity to achieve the transformation you seek. With our 30-day unconditional guarantee, you have nothing to lose and everything to gain.

What You'll Receive:

- In-depth video modules (2.5 hours of expert guidance)
    - 68-page comprehensive workbook
    - Bonus ebook: "How Can I Trust You Again?"
    - 24/7 access to the program
    - 30-day unconditional guarantee
    - Strictly confidential participation

By combining the insights from the book with the immersive experience of the Affair Recovery Workshop, you'll be equipped with the knowledge, tools, and support needed to overcome the devastation of infidelity and build a stronger, more resilient marriage.

Take action now and claim your 30% discount on the Affair Recovery Workshop. Visit **www.AffairRecoveryWorkshop.com** and use the coupon code **WORKSHOP30** to start your transformative journey to-day. Your satisfaction is 100% guaranteed.

Wishing you all the best on your path to healing and rediscovering the love and connection you deserve,

Jeffrey D. Murrah, LPC, LCDC